MODELLERS GUIDE
TO THE LNER

MODELLERS' GUIDE TO THE LNER

David Adair

Patrick Stephens
Wellingborough, Northamptonshire

Cover illustrations
Front, top to bottom Class 'A3' 'Pacific' No 97
Humorist sporting experimental smoke deflectors
and double chimney; kit-built twin third/third
articulated coach set; a modified Hornby model
becomes Class 'A4' 'Pacific' No 24 *Kingfisher;* a
selection of goods wagons showing fine attention to
detail. **Back, top left** Carefully-detailed models of
a 'Toad D' brake van and cattle van. **Top right** A
former LNER station scene rich in detail for the
observant modeller. **Bottom left** A typical NBR
signalbox at Alloa. **Bottom right** Close-up of the
front of a beautifully detailed Class 'B12' 4-6-0.

First published September 1987

British Library Cataloguing in Publication

Adair, David
Modellers' guide to the LNER
1. London and North Eastern Railway —
History   2. Railroads — Models
3. Railroads — Great Britain —
Rolling-Stock
I. Title
625.2'0941   TF197

ISBN 0-85059-831-1

*Patrick Stephens Limited is part of the
Thorsons Publishing Group*

Printed and bound in Great Britain

1 3 5 7 9 10 8 6 4 2

Dedication
To all my friends and fellow modellers who ever knew a quickening of the pulse at the sight of a blue or green locomotive at the head of a rake of teak coaches, and who managed to translate their regard into model form.

Disclaimer

Throughout this book mention is made of various manufacturers and their products. The author wishes to disclaim any business or commercial connection with them whatsoever and writes of them only as a user.

Contents

Preface

Born in 1937 not a small piece of ballast's throw from the former NBR station at Alloa, Clackmannanshire, Scotland, amongst the first sounds I heard must be included the shrill whistle of locomotives, the clanging of wagon buffers and the distinctive wheeze of Westinghouse brake pumps. I have often been asked where my interest in railways came from, a not unreasonable question when it is known that almost all of my working life has been spent in aviation.

Looking back I suppose if anyone is to blame, and the question is sometimes accusative as well as inquisitive, then I have to answer 'Marconi'. My parents owned a wireless set powered by an acid filled glass jar known as an accumulator. As a youngster it was my job every few days to take this to the local radio shop to be recharged. The shop itself was hard by the station and during the hour or so it took to charge up, what better way to spend the time than by sitting on the wall and watching the trains go by? So it was that from quite a tender age I became fascinated by the steam railway and familiar with many classes of LNER locomotives. As the majority of my family lived in Edinburgh I often travelled by train to the city, crossing the River Forth either by the mighty Forth Bridge or its lesser known partner at Alloa.

Once in Edinburgh whole new vistas opened up. Pacifics in both streamlined and unstreamlined form, Scotts, Glens, Directors, B1s, myriads of 0-6-0s and tank locomotives delighted a youthful eye. Many happy hours were spent at the 'Waverley' or in Prince's Street Gardens and so it was that a life-long passion for railways and in particular big locomotives was born.

A family move to England in 1948 provided residence alongside the former Cheshire Lines Committee tracks where the motive power was again mainly LNER. No big locomotives here alas, but later the Royal Air Force, in a moment of uncharacteristic generosity, saw fit to provide a posting to a radar station a few miles from Peterborough and within easy cycling distance of the east coast main line. A return to civilian life and marriage saw residence again established alongside the CLC (Cheshire Lines Committee) and later the old London–Manchester main line now wholly devoid of steam.

Like many railway enthusiasts then I suspect that my interest in and regard for a particular railway came about because of accidents of history and geography rather than by deliberate choice. Gradually all that seemed familiar and dependable was swept away so that my thoughts turned to perpetuating my memories of the LNER in model form.

So it was that in 1964 I found myself amongst a group of like-minded individuals who in 1965 were to found the LNER Society, later retitled the LNER Study Group. Membership not only gave access to a host of new friends and a wealth of hitherto untapped information but the chance to serve on the committee in various posts including that of Chairman. Presently taking time out to 'ride the cushions' I have written many constructional articles for the model railway press, attended exhibitions with my own layouts and continue to practise the enjoyable art of railway modelling.

Acknowledgements

This book could not have been written from the knowledge possessed by one individual. Detailed information has been gathered over many years and from many sources and my general gratitude goes to all who contributed to my own store of knowledge.

My particular thanks are due to Geoff Barlow of Poole for loaning some stock photographed for this book and for keeping me supplied with modellers' bits and pieces for more years than either of us care to recall. The majority of photographs presented here are the work of Mike Godden of Bournemouth who exercised his skill and patience on my behalf, and to whom I am grateful. My special thanks must go too to the various members of the LNER Study Group for their generous support and help over the years and to Maureen Dougan for the hours she spent typing up my scratch notes into a usable format. Lastly, but by no means least, thank you to my long-suffering wife for her forbearance in living in what must have occasionally seemed to be a miniature version of Doncaster Plant.

David Adair
Ringwood, December 1986

About the book

The idea for writing this book came to me when I was thumbing through a number of folders containing railway notes, drawings, photographs and articles collected over a 25 year period. This collection, together with a large number of carefully selected books, forms a good source of reference. The problem is of course that it can sometimes take a considerable time to locate a particular piece of information. How useful it would be if much of the basic information could be found within the covers of one book.

It is appropriate that this book should be written in 1986 when the LNER Study Group is 21 years old. Many members have published articles and others have written railway books during those years. These will continue to appear from time to time and together with the excellent series of books, 'Locomotives of the LNER', currently being produced by the Railway Correspondence & Travel Society, the LNER modeller is provided with more information than ever before.

The relentless march of time was also considered. The LNER can still be remembered by many of us but if interest in and enthusiasm for the line is to continue than it must be vested in those who come after; those who have never seen a 'Gresley' in full cry or a 2-8-0 barking its way up a long drag at the head of a line of goods wagons. Some readers may also be new to the hobby of railway modelling so that the purpose of this book is two-fold. Firstly it is to provide a source of ready reference for the established modeller and secondly to suggest to the newcomer various ways in which they might reproduce good LNER models. Some of the information may seem, to those already skilled as model makers, very basic and rather obvious but I would ask them to be patient and remember that we all had to start somewhere. There has never been much merit in continually re-inventing the wheel and much of what is written here regarding tools and methods illustrates that which has been learned the hard way both by myself and my colleagues. Where possible information has been made available on subjects not covered at length elsewhere and reference to other useful reading material is made in Appendix E to this book.

If, in years to come, the model railway scene is to include a representation of the LNER in all its glory and its grime then it will be due to the efforts of the many authors and draughtsmen who have given so freely of their time and expertise to make their information available to others. Hopefully this book will add to that source and help to generate and maintain enthusiasm in some measure so that the spirit of a once proud railway will live on for many years to come.

Introduction

It is many years since the last steam engine ran in regular revenue earning service on British Railways and almost forty years since the London & North Eastern Railway lost its unique identity, being absorbed along with the LMS, SR and GWR into the nationalized railway system. To those who never experienced it, it is difficult now to imagine the railways in their prime. Marshalling yards containing hundreds and hundreds of freight vehicles, locomotive depots with line upon line of steam locomotives and main lines which enjoyed the continual passage of trains are now nothing but a memory.

That all this had to change was brought about by the passage of time, lack of capital investment and the debilitating effect of war. Industries which had once supplied the railways with trade were to fall into decline and so the railways became the victim of circumstance and political whim. That which remains today, although technically advanced in many respects, represents only a thin shadow of the system as it once was.

There are now railway modellers, quite adult, for whom not only the existence of the 'Big Four', but also the day to day operation of the steam railway, is beyond living memory. As a subject for the railway modeller the LNER has always been an attractive line, but not always easily translated into model form using ready to run items or by the use of kits. For this reason it has been followed in the main by a few devotees and has never enjoyed the almost universal popularity of the GWR which has long been supported by the model manufacturers. No doubt some modellers will have been put off by the need to simulate the beautiful teak finish used by the LNER for most of its coaching stock.

Running from its London termini to the far north of Scotland with lines extending into such unexpected places as North Wales, the LNER was called upon to provide for a great variety of industrial and social needs. Coal, fish, iron, steel, general merchandise, agricultural products, livestock and the operation of an extensive dock system and merchant fleet all combined to make the LNER a line full of interest and contrast. Always short of money, the LNER had to plan its modernization programme with selection and care. This is one reason why, right up to the end of 1948, a great variety of locomotive and rolling stock types could still be seen, many of them dating back to well before 1923.

Standardization of design, especially when applied to locomotives, was not generally widespread. Passenger stock was equally varied with, on the one hand, passengers being conveyed in speed and comfort in the latest design of carriage and, on the other, by somewhat slower trains made up of a variety of pre-grouping stock which served on many a branch line until these services ceased. Indeed it is this very diversity which makes the LNER so attractive and yet quite daunting as a prototype for the modeller.

Within this book it is intended to give a broad brush picture of the railway, its traffic and connected activities. More importantly it is hoped to show how anyone, given a modicum of skill and patience, might reproduce a representative section of the LNER or its operation of his own choosing. Additional items can often be made by the judicious rebuilding of existing items or by cross kitting. All of this can be undertaken without major workshop facilities, a degree in engineering, or the dexterity of a surgeon.

Throughout this book little reference is made to the relative merits of one scale or gauge over another. This decision is the prerogative of the individual, being influenced by such considerations as the time and space available and not least by the amount of money that can be spared. However, for ease of presentation and where possible, drawings are done to a commonly-used model railway scale (4 or 7mm to foot) where this fits into the format of the book.

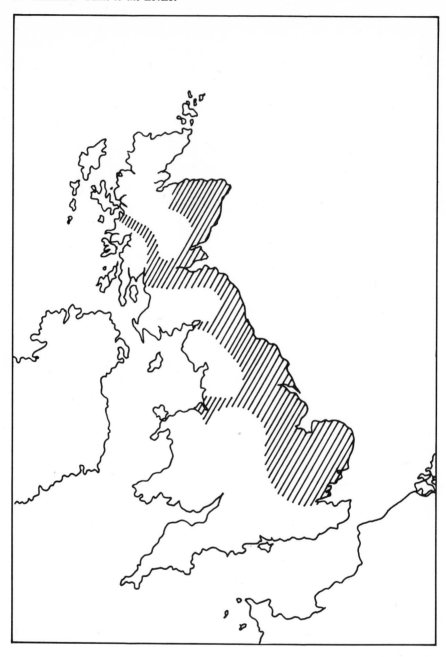

Map showing the area served by the lines of the London & North Eastern Railway.

Chapter 1

The LNER

The London & North Eastern Railway began its existence on 1 January 1923 as a result of the Railway Act of 1921, which received the Royal Assent on 19 August of that year. The Act set up the four mainline railway companies otherwise known as the 'Big Four'. The others were:

The London, Midland & Scottish Railway (LMS)
The Southern Railway (SR)
The Great Western Railway (GWR)

The latter was the only one to retain its original title, expanding its interests by acquiring a number of smaller railways, mainly in Wales.

The LNER was second largest to the LMS but in financial terms was the least successful of the four companies. By comparison with the LMS the LNER had 93 per cent of its route mileage, 72 per cent of its staff but only around 66 per cent of its traffic receipts. It is something of a paradox therefore that the LNER should also have been a major innovator in so many aspects of railway operation and development. The new railway was formed by the amalgamation of the following companies, together with a number of lines that were jointly owned or operated:

The Great Northern Railway (GNR)
The North Eastern Railway (NER)
The North British Railway (NBR)
The Great North of Scotland Railway (GNoSR)
The Great Central Railway (GCR)
The Great Eastern Railway (GER)

The North Eastern Railway had, just prior to the grouping, absorbed the former Hull & Barnsley Railway (H&BR) on 1 April 1922.

Thus it was that the LNER found itself with a total route mileage of 6,675 miles and the need to manage a wide range of traffic and facilities. Amongst the early problems to exercise the minds of the new Board of Directors was the choice of a suitable name for the company. This decision was obviously something of a public relations exercise as well as an attempt to pacify the larger members of the group some of whom considered themselves a definite cut above the others. Whatever was chosen by way of initials, the effect would have important consequences, not least the amount of repainting required as well as new company letter heads and vast quantities of forms. The cost of any change was never going to be small, the cost of a major change could have been astronomical.

Amongst the names considered were The Great North Railway Company and

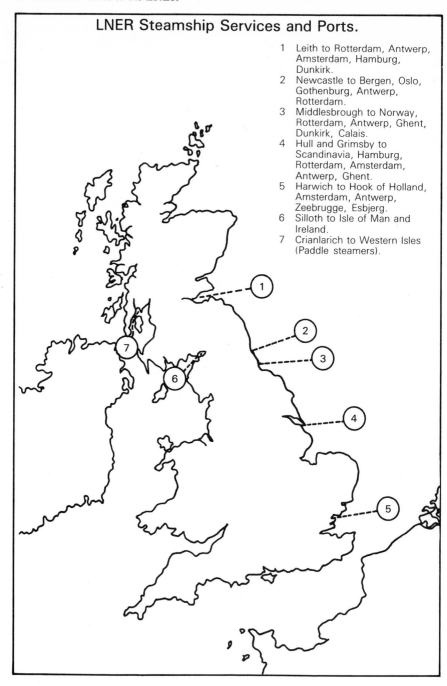

LNER Steamship Services and Ports.

1 Leith to Rotterdam, Antwerp, Amsterdam, Hamburg, Dunkirk.
2 Newcastle to Bergen, Oslo, Gothenburg, Antwerp, Rotterdam.
3 Middlesbrough to Norway, Rotterdam, Antwerp, Ghent, Dunkirk, Calais.
4 Hull and Grimsby to Scandinavia, Hamburg, Rotterdam, Amsterdam, Antwerp, Ghent.
5 Harwich to Hook of Holland, Amsterdam, Antwerp, Zeebrugge, Esbjerg.
6 Silloth to Isle of Man and Ireland.
7 Crianlarich to Western Isles (Paddle steamers).

The North East Railway Company. There seemed to be a curious reluctance to acknowledge that a major part of the line was actually in Scotland! After much discussion and correspondence the title adopted was The London & North Eastern Railway Company. This was originally applied to locomotive stock using the initials L&NER, but before too long the ampersand was left out and LNER was universally applied. No doubt even a minor modification to style such as this resulted in a considerable saving overall in both paint and effort. For freight stock the plain and rather uninspired initials NE were used with the big advantage that the huge stock of former North Eastern Railway vehicles could be left alone as they already carried these initials.

There are many excellent reference books on the constituent companies that went to make up the LNER. However to give a better overall understanding of the operation some general detail is given here as it affected the LNER upon its foundation.

The Great Northern Railway

Total route mileage including joint and leased lines: 1,051
Rolling stock (passenger and freight): 45,055
Locomotives: 1,359
From its major London terminus at King's Cross, opened in October 1852, the main line ran northwards to Shaftholme Junction near Doncaster. At this point it made an end on junction with the North Eastern Railway, thus forming the southern end of the east coast main line. It was also the southern partner in the provision of the East Coast Joint Service. A line built for speed between major centres of population and trade, it was a considerable rival to the London & North Western Railway and the Midland Railway. The GNR also had lines in Lincolnshire, Nottinghamshire, and the West Riding of Yorkshire. A significant part of its operation involved the transhipment of coal as well as handling traffic generated by other parts of the system. The main line included the famous racing stretch between Grantham and Peterborough.

Of all the constituent companies it was the only one not to operate any major port facilities. It did however handle a very heavy suburban traffic generated to the north of London. Leaving aside the solitary 'Great Bear' of the GWR it was also the first railway to introduce the 4-6-2 Pacific type of locomotive which was to stand the LNER in such good stead in the years to come when that type of locomotive formed the back-bone of the high speed mainline services.

The North Eastern Railway

Total route mileage, including 106 gained from the previously absorbed Hull & Barnsley Railway: 1,866
Rolling stock (passenger and freight): 131,844
Locomotives, including 138 gained from the previously absorbed Hull & Barnsley Railway: 2,156
Running northwards from Shaftholme Junction the NER main line passed through York and Newcastle then onwards to Berwick upon Tweed where it made

an end on junction with the North British Railway. The NER also enjoyed running powers over NBR metals to Edinburgh. Within its compass were the heavily industrialized areas of north-east England and it moved a greater tonnage of coal and minerals than any other railway in the United Kingdom. The extensive coalfields through which it ran accounted for the fact that it owned the largest single wagon fleet to come under LNER ownership, a great many of which were bottom discharge hopper wagons of 20 tons capacity. It is also interesting to note that there were no private owner wagons registered with the NER. The owner and operator of extensive port facilities, the NER expanded in this field with the acquisition of similar facilities previously owned by the Hull & Barnsley Railway. A heavy suburban traffic was generated around the industrial towns. The NER was the second partner in the development and working of the East Coast Joint Service.

The North British Railway

Total route mileage: 1,378
Rolling stock (passenger and freight): 62,546
Locomotives: 1,075

The North British Railway was geographically an extensive network. Its main line continued the north to south theme, running from Berwick upon Tweed via Edinburgh to Kinnaber Junction, thence to Aberdeen, the final 38 miles of which was over Caledonian Railway metals. It had another main line running east to west along the Forth/Clyde Valley serving the industrial belt as well as the cities of Edinburgh and Glasgow. Northwards from Glasgow yet another important line led into the West Highland network. Included in its route to Aberdeen were two major water crossings via the impressive bridges over the Firth of Forth and the Firth of Tay. To the south and west of Edinburgh another line joined that city to Carlisle over the Waverley route. This enabled direct traffic interchange to take place with the Midland Railway and to this end a number of coaching vehicles to Midland design were operated under the title of Midland and North British Joint Stock. Owners and operators of extensive port facilities, the NBR was the third partner, along with the GNR and NER, in the provision of East Coast Joint Services.

The Great North of Scotland Railway

Route mileage: 334
Rolling stock (passenger and freight): 4,493
Locomotives: 122

Although physically separated from its southern counterparts, the GNoSR was, nevertheless, always considered to be part of the total east coast railway system. Running northwards and westwards from Aberdeen it served the remainder of north-east Scotland. Agricultural produce, fish and tourists, together with the ingredients for the 'water of life', were all carried by the GNoSR. Like its Scottish partner it also traversed some of the finest scenery in Scotland and boasted royal connections in transporting members of the royal family on their journeys to Balmoral.

The Great Central Railway

Route mileage: 855
Rolling stock (passenger and freight): 41,020
Locomotives: 1,358
The Great Central Railway operated in two distinct areas. From the former Manchester, Sheffield & Lincolnshire Railway it inherited the heavily used trans-Pennine route. Largely a freight route, it carried large quantities of coal throughout the Lancashire/Yorkshire industrial belt. It also owned the massive port of Immingham on the River Humber. This had been completed in 1912 at a cost of £2,600,000.

The London extension of the GCR ran from Annesley southwards through Nottingham and Leicester to the terminus at Marylebone, opened in 1899. This line was unique in that it was the only major railway to be built *into* London. It was hoped that this would compete successfully for passenger traffic with the lines of the London & North Western Railway and the Midland Railway. The GCR also participated with the GNR and the MR in the operation of the Cheshire Lines Committee (CLC), including the provision of the motive power.

The Great Eastern Railway

Route mileage: 1,191
Rolling stock (passenger and freight): 35,652
Locomotives: 1,336
The Great Eastern Railway served the largely agricultural area of East Anglia from its London terminus at Liverpool Street. It also worked a major coal traffic through Peterborough and March mainly into the London area. As well as working passenger traffic to and from the popular coastal resorts and ports the GER worked a highly intensive passenger traffic on its suburban lines around London. Services of a more prestigious nature were worked to the port of Harwich by boat trains made up of coaching stock allocated specifically for that purpose. Connections with royalty could again be claimed when the royal family visited Sandringham.

Joint lines and services

A number of lines were jointly owned, operated, or leased by the LNER constituent companies and other railways. A few examples are given here.

Midland & Great Northern Joint Railway

Owned in equal shares by the Midland Railway and the Great Northern Railway, the M&GNR had 183 route miles of track. The railway was operated with its own rolling stock and owned 101 locomotives as well as its own works at Melton Constable. On 1 October 1936 the sole responsibility for ownership passed to the LNER and the surviving locomotives and rolling stock were taken into LNER stock.

Great Northern & Great Eastern Joint Line
This 123 mile line became wholly owned and operated by the LNER upon the formation of the latter, as did the West Riding & Grimsby Joint Line with a much smaller route mileage of 31½.

East Coast Joint Service
In order to facilitate the smooth travel of passengers using the east coast through route, the Great Northern Railway, the North Eastern Railway and the North British Railway jointly built and operated a number of coaching vehicles for this purpose. Known as East Coast Joint Stock it was lettered ECJS, carried the coat of arms of the amalgamation and was numbered in its own series. This stock remained a separate entity within the LNER until that company ceased to exist and new stock allocated to that service were numbered accordingly.

Cheshire Lines Committee
This railway had a route mileage of 143 and was equally owned by the Great Northern Railway, the Great Central Railway and the Midland Railway. After the grouping the ownership became two-thirds LNER and one-third LMS. Locomotives for the CLC services formerly supplied by the GCR continued to be supplied by the LNER.

Sources of traffic and management

In 1923 the railways of Britain enjoyed a virtual monopoly as a means of transporting passengers and freight all over the country, the latter at the expense of the canals. Air travel was posing no serious challenge and the coming threat from road transport was barely recognized. The joining together of a number of well established railways to form the LNER was to provide a service to the traveller and the industrialist never equalled since. As a result the LNER found itself catering for a great many needs within the United Kingdom including the operation of an extensive shipping fleet, having inherited a large number of port and dock facilities.

By far the major fuel of the time was coal. The LNER was required to move vast tonnages not only for its own use but also to serve the domestic and industrial user as well as a thriving export trade. The areas of heavy industry which the line encompassed produced their own traffic both in raw materials and finished products.

From East Anglia came livestock and agricultural produce, from the Midlands and Yorkshire came coal and the products of heavy industry. From the North-east came more coal, the output of heavy industry, fish and an increasing mineral traffic for a growing chemical industry. North of the border came more of the same from coal, industry, fish, agricultural produce and livestock. The many centres of population generated a constant demand in passenger traffic between and around those centres.

To meet these demands the LNER opened its account with 6,675 route miles of track and some 7,406 locomotives of which 7,383 were steam. Passenger stock consisted of 20,156 vehicles whilst freight vehicles and departmental stock totalled 300,454 units. The offices of the Chairman, Company Secretary and the boardroom were at Marylebone whilst those of the Chief General Manager and the Chief Accountant were at King's Cross. The management of such a vast organization could not be undertaken lightly and to facilitate division of the line into manageable areas the following organization was set up.

Southern Area
This was comprised of the lines of the former Great Northern Railway, Great Eastern Railway and Great Central Railway and had its headquarters at Liverpool Street.

North Eastern Area
Comprised of the lines of the former North Eastern Railway, it had its headquarters at York.

Southern Scottish Area
Comprised of the lines of the former North British Railway, it had its headquarters at Edinburgh.

Northern Scottish Area
Comprised of the lines of the former Great North of Scotland Railway and part of the NBR, it had its headquarters at Aberdeen.

Both the Southern and Northern Scottish Areas came under the control of the General Manager, Scotland.

This division of general management into areas as opposed to 'whole line' was a shrewd move. Whilst ensuring adherence to official policy it allowed the staff of the constituent railways to feel that they belonged rather than having become faceless members of a conglomeration. Working conditions were often appalling, hours long and wages poor but employees could be fiercely loyal when 'their' railway was under discussion. This was especially true the further away from London the scene of operations became. Many a former NBR or GNoSR employee never considered himself to be working for the LNER, let alone British Railways.

This division into virtually autonomous areas, together with the lack of capital for major renewal programmes combined to make the LNER an interesting line for modellers although it must, at times, have produced nightmares for the operating staff. With one or two notable exceptions each area operated the locomotives and rolling stock it previously owned. Even when standard designs did appear in quantity they very often simply released existing stock for less arduous duties. So it was that upon the foundation of British Railways in 1948 there existed on the LNER many locomotives and pieces of rolling stock which were still of pre-grouping design. The LNER might have set itself high standards, but a railway of high standardization it most certainly was not.

LNER numbering policy
Reference has already been made to the implications of a choice of name for the LNER and the effect such a choice would have upon the repainting of locomotives and rolling stock. No less problematical was what to do about numbering the total stock as each of the constituent companies had numbered according to their own system. Naturally such a scheme could not be organized overnight, let alone

implemented. Therefore the first full scheme did not come into use until 1924. While the new scheme was being drafted certain measures were put into effect in the interim.

Locomotives

Not only did the LNER inherit a great many locomotives, it also inherited the working practices of its predecessors including all the variations in the ways they numbered their locomotives. Broadly speaking this fell into three categories: taking the next available number at the end of the list; taking numbers now vacant in the list or transferring much older locomotives to a duplicate list and reusing their numbers; and allocating block numbers to a particular class or wheel arrangement. The GNR, GCR and GER used both of the first two methods without really favouring either one whereas the GER did show an inclination towards filling gaps in the original list. The NER also followed the first two methods but had discarded the use of a duplicate list some time previously. The NBR on the other hand carried out block transfers to the duplicate list every six months whilst the GNoSR filled gaps and also carried out occasional transfers to a duplicate list. In order to identify locomotives on the duplicate list the different companies again used different methods. One involved adding a small suffix letter to the existing number, for example, A for GNR and GNoSR or B in the case of the GCR. The other involved renumbering those locomotives transferred to the list. At grouping the GNR had 26 locos on their duplicate list, the GCR 106, the GER 4, the NER none, the NBR 200 and the GNoSR 7.

Whatever method was going to be used by the LNER something needed to be done quickly. To quote just one example there were sixteen cases where no less than seven different locos were running with the same number. In September 1923 a scheme was introduced to differentiate between numbers by using a suffix letter, as follows:

N for locos ex-GNR
D for locos ex-NER
B for locos ex-NBR
S for locos ex-GNoSR
E for locos ex-GER
C for locos ex-GCR

Unfortunately this did not prove to be the ideal answer as duplication still took place, as for example the suffix B being used on former GCR duplicate list locomotives and also on former NBR locomotives. Meanwhile the 126 new locomotives constructed in 1923 were given numbers in the series used by the company that ordered them. This method was in use for almost six months until the revised renumbering scheme was brought in on 6 February 1924. This new scheme involved the addition of a figure in front of the original number to indicate the line of origin:

NER absorbed stock retained their existing numbers with the exception of the former H&BR locomotives which had already been renumbered by the NER by adding 3,000 to their old numbers. They were now to be totally renumbered in the

block 2405–2542.
GNR absorbed stock: 3,000 added to existing numbers
GCR absorbed stock: 5,000 added to existing numbers
GER absorbed stock: 7,000 added to existing numbers
NBR absorbed stock: 9,000 added to existing numbers
GNoSR absorbed stock: 6,800 added to existing numbers

Locomotives constructed between 1924 and 1941 either to existing or new designs were numbered by filling the gaps in the original list. All of this led eventually to a numbering system of which perhaps the kindest thing that can be said of it is that it was haphazard. Before leaving the 1924 scheme however it is necessary to look again at the locomotives on the duplicate lists.

The NER did not operate a duplicate list whilst the GNoSR, although it allocated numbers, never actually applied them and their list was cleared by 1926 in any case. The GNR and the GER did the obvious thing and added 3,000 and 7,000 respectively. For some unexplained reason the GCR chose to allocate numbers 6402–6494 but the NBR dreamed up a scheme all of its own. It began by filling up the blanks in its capital list and then allocated 9927–10050 to those locomotives that could not be accommodated. However when only twelve locomotives had actually been renumbered in this way, by July 1924, they reverted to adding 9,000.

Sundry renumberings took place from time to time but the next significant renumbering took place in 1942. This was to clear the numbers 8301–8900 inclusive to make way for the then new Thompson Class B1. Always intended to be a numerically large class, the majority of them did not appear until after 1945.

In 1943 the then Chief Mechanical Engineer, Edward Thompson, introduced the first real attempt at a systematic numbering scheme. A number of locomotives were renumbered but wartime conditions were hardly ideal for this exercise and so the scheme was postponed until the end of hostilities. When peace came in 1945 a completely new and systematic renumbering scheme was drawn up and the first locomotive was renumbered on Sunday 13 January 1946. The whole exercise was completed in just over twelve months. The method now employed meant that whole classes were numbered in sequence although within a class new numbers were not necessarily allocated in the order of building. After 1948 British Railways added 60,000 to all ex-LNER locomotive numbers although not all were carried, some being withdrawn before they were repainted.

Coaching stock
As with the locomotive stock a similarly confused start was made in the renumbering of passenger carrying vehicles and passenger brake vans. The 1923 scheme intended that all absorbed vehicles would retain their original numbers but a letter suffix would denote the line from which they originated or to which they had been reallocated. New stock already ordered to the design of constituent companies was to be numbered into the existing series. These suffixes were allocated as follows: N for GNR; Y for NER; B for NBR; S for GNoSR; C for GCR; and E for GER. New stock to the LNER standard designs was to be numbered in a series beginning at 10,000. The addition of a suffix letter would

indicate the section to which these were allocated. Throughout this scheme no attempt was made to indicate the type of vehicles by the allocation of a particular numbering series.

By April 1925 it was realized that this was a far from satisfactory scheme and a revised version was introduced. This did away with the suffix letter but added a prefix number to the existing number to denote the line of origin. Even this could cause confusion however as vehicles were renumbered on being transferred from one section to another. The prefix additions were as follows: 1 for ECJS stock; 2 for NER stock; 3 for NBR stock; 4 for GNR stock; 5 for GCR stock; 6 for GER stock; and 7 for the GNoSR stock. New standard stock was allocated a number beginning with the digit denoting its operating section. Some attempt was also made under the 1925 scheme to allocate blocks of numbers to specific types of vehicles. However, these were not discrete number blocks. There were four categories:

Passenger coaches and passenger brake vans

Non-common user vans

Horse boxes and special cattle trucks

Carriage trucks

Whilst this served to limit the total number series it did mean that vehicles from each group could and did carry the same number. Once again a somewhat haphazard system which remained in use until 1946. By this date a completely new and much more logical system had been devised. This scheme was introduced at the same time as the establishment of a centralized rolling stock control based at York. It allocated discrete blocks of numbers based upon vehicle type, for example, 9000 upwards covered catering vehicles. It is interesting to note that the new numbers were allocated against all of the previously existing numbers. This meant that the new list contained several gaps which would have been used but for the fact that the vehicles no longer existed, usually having met their end due to enemy action.

Following nationalization in 1948 a prefix letter was added (E1136) but when British Railways began to introduce its own standard stock a suffix letter was also added to indicate the region of origin (E1136E).

Freight stock

Each of the constituent companies operated its own scheme for wagon numbering. In the main this consisted of re-using numbers as they became vacant or adding to the end of the list. The withdrawal of vehicles through old age or accident damage occurred in a random fashion so that numbers were re-allocated in a totally random fashion. The NER, because of its huge and still expanding fleet of wagons, had already decided that it did not wish to number vehicles using six digits. From about 1908 until 1922 the vehicle was identified by a prefix letter followed by only three digits. For clarity certain letters were omitted from the list. H, I, O, P and Q were not used so that the letter Z would have been reached in 1922. Rather than employ double letters, from then on a return to the use of six digits was made, the numbers 110001 to 12900 being allocated. It can be understood that with such a large fleet involved it was some time into the post-grouping era before all were renumbered. Freight stock gained from the Hull & Barnsley Railway had the prefix HB added to their existing numbers.

When considering a renumbering scheme the LNER wisely decided to leave the NER vehicles as they were and increased the existing numbers of the other constituent companies as follows:

GNR vehicles: 400,000 added to existing numbers
GCR vehicles: 500,000 added to existing numbers
GER vehicles: 600,000 added to existing numbers
NBR vehicles: 700,000 added to existing numbers
GNS vehicles: 800,000 added to existing numbers

New vehicles built early on in the existence of the LNER were of course to pre-grouping design and whilst it appears that it was the intention to number these by extending the NER list some confusion occurred. Certainly some vehicles were treated in this way but others were numbered in the lists of the pre-grouping companies to which they owed their origin. Eventually those placed on the NER list, if to a pre-grouping design, were renumbered.

From 1929 the LNER abandoned the use of vacant numbers and began to number in sequence. However with the exception of relatively small batches of vehicles built by the LNER, or for them by outside contractors, it never adopted the policy of allocating specific blocks to particular groups of vehicles. Mixed batches that arrived for painting simply joined the line and were numbered as they came along.

Departmental stock

Under this title all the constituents operated non-revenue earning stock for their own use. This usually consisted of old vehicles long past earning their bread and butter but with a limited life left. For a few years after the grouping they were left to carry their original numbers but by the early thirties some at least were being renumbered into a new six figure series, the first two digits of which indicated the constituent areas to which they were allocated. The prefixes were:

North Eastern Area: 20
Southern Area — GN Section: 47
                  GC Section: 54
                  GE Section: 63
Southern Scottish Area: 77
Northern Scottish Area: 88

Having read about the schemes and counter schemes employed for numbering locomotives and passenger stock it will come as no surprise to learn that well could hardly be left alone. In 1939 a new scheme was introduced. Once again six digits were used but this time they could be interpreted. The first digit was always 9 whilst the second indicated the area to which the vehicle belonged. The third digit indicated the operating department whilst the last three digits were the number. The full list of prefixes for the revised scheme was:

North Eastern Area: 90
Southern Area — GN Section: 94
                  GC Section: 95

GE Section: 96
Southern Scottish Area: 97
Northern Scottish Area: 98
The third digits were:
Engineers: 0
Loco Dept: 1
Workshops: 2
Stores: 3

From the modeller's point of view the disadvantage of this system is that the number gives no indication of the origin of the vehicle if it is newly transferred from revenue stock or transferred between areas.

The foregoing is of necessity an abbreviated account of the formation of the LNER and some of the early problems with which it had to contend. The message for the modeller, however, is loud and clear: be careful and use good, captioned photographs as reference material. The period 1923 to 1925 is that which contains the most uncertainty but is, nevertheless, an interesting one to model, being full of variety. Just how much variety will become apparent when the chapter on liveries is reached. Fortunately, and as already mentioned, there are many excellent publications available which give chapter and verse on locomotives, coaches and freight stock. (See Appendix E.)

Chapter 2

Locomotives

The modeller of today shares one problem with the LNER in 1923; that is to try and assess the bewildering array of locomotives in their various classes and sub-divisions of those classes and to suit these to traffic needs. Never a well off railway, the LNER operated many of the pre-grouping types for all of its existence which says much for the soundness of the original designs. All of the railways of Britain had suffered badly during the First World War; the shortage of money, manpower, materials and maintenance had all combined to leave the railways in a run down state. Recovery had begun but it was slow and the constituent companies of the LNER suffered as much as any others.

As a result, in 1923, although the company was well off for locomotives in some areas of operation it was less so in others. The newly appointed Chief Mechanical Engineer, H.N. Gresley as he then was, set about rectifying this situation to achieve a better balance of motive power throughout the system. Although he was to become a world renowed railway engineer in his own right, Gresley was also capable of recognizing the worth of his fellow engineers. As a result, and to save the time needed to introduce new designs, the LNER continued to build locomotives to pre-grouping designs. The resulting locomotives however often

A BEC white metal kit on a Triang chassis modifed to represent a Class D11/2, the LNER-built version of a pre-grouping GCR design. With lowered cab and boiler mountings to fit the Scottish loading gauge, the model sports the plain black livery and 'economy' style of lettering. Note also the traditional NBR style of painting names on splashers.

strayed away from their line of origin. For example the 24 'Improved Directors', based upon the previous GCR design were all allocated to the lines of the former NBR. Another solution was to transfer existing designs so that a number of Class B12 locomotives were sent from their native GER to the former lines of the GNoSR. Such decisions were not reached without due consideration of other factors such as restrictions on axle loading, the length of turntables or run-round loops for example.

The LNER was to continue to build new locomotives and rebuild others throughout its existence. Some of these spent their whole lives in one area, some

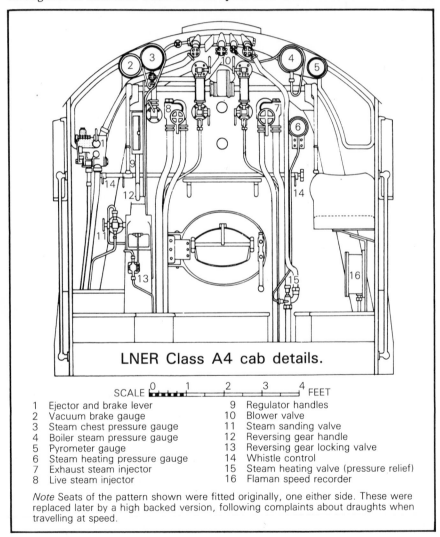

LNER Class A4 cab details.

SCALE 0 1 2 3 4 FEET

1	Ejector and brake lever	9	Regulator handles
2	Vacuum brake gauge	10	Blower valve
3	Steam chest pressure gauge	11	Steam sanding valve
4	Boiler steam pressure gauge	12	Reversing gear handle
5	Pyrometer gauge	13	Reversing gear locking valve
6	Steam heating pressure gauge	14	Whistle control
7	Exhaust steam injector	15	Steam heating valve (pressure relief)
8	Live steam injector	16	Flaman speed recorder

Note Seats of the pattern shown were fitted originally, one either side. These were replaced later by a high backed version, following complaints about draughts when travelling at speed.

even allocated to one shed. Others of course made several moves and there were also limited exchanges of locomotives between areas. This happened, for example, in the case of shunting locomotives where English types were sent north and Scottish types were sent south for trial periods.

Locomotive classification system

Although the constituent companies had all used a system for classifying groups of locomotives these systems were all different. Letters, letters and numbers and numbers only were variously used but none of the systems gave precise information about the locomotives within any group. In 1923 Gresley tasked Doncaster to devise a system for common use and the proposed scheme was approved in September of that year. It was based upon that previously employed by the GNR. Generally tender locomotives were dealt with first, followed by tank locomotives. Within this broad framework individual classes were dealt with according to their line of origin in the sequence GNR, GCR, GER, NER, NBR and GNoSR. A further refinement was to group locomotives in sequence according to wheel arrangements beginning with six coupled passenger, then four coupled passenger, six coupled goods, eight coupled goods and miscellaneous. Twenty two letters were used in the initial scheme to define wheel arrangements, as follows:

A 4-6-2	B 4-6-0	C 4-4-2	D 4-4-0	E 2-4-0	F 2-4-2
G 0-4-4	H 4-4-4	J 0-6-0	K 2-6-0	L 2-6-4	M 0-6-4
N 0-6-3	O 2-8-0	P 2-8-2	Q 0-8-0	R 0-8-2	S 0-8-4
T 4-8-0	X 2-2-4 and 4-2-2		Y 0-4-0 and miscellaneous types.		

The letter I was never used, but U, V and W, whilst not in the original list, were subsequently used:

U 2-8-0 + 0-8-2   V 2-6-2   W 4-6-4

Within each wheel arrangement, and in the sequence of companies already mentioned, further classification was based upon wheel diameter, the largest usually coming first although there were, as ever, minor exceptions to this rule. A few locomotives were never included in the new system either because they were already very close to withdrawal or because, in at least one instance, they appear to have been forgotten. A certain degree of foresight was also used in compiling the list to allow for planned expansion and the introduction of new designs. The full list of classes in 1923 was:

Class A: 1, 2, 5, 6, 7.
Class B: 1, 2, 3, 4, 5, 6, 7, 8, 9, 12, 13, 14, 15, 16.
Class C: 1, 2, 4, 5, 6, 7, 8, 10, 11, 12, 13, 14, 15, 16.
Class D: 1, 2, 3, 4, 5, 6, 7, 8, 9, 10, 11, 12, 13, 14, 15, 16, 17, 18, 19, 20, 21, 22, 23, 24, 25, 26, 27, 28, 29, 30, 31, 32, 33, 34, 35, 36, 38, 39, 40, 41, 42, 43, 44, 45, 46, 47, 48, 50, 51.
Class E: 1, 2, 4, 5, 7, 8.
Class F: 1, 2, 3, 4, 5, 6, 7, 8.
Class G: 1, 2, 3, 4, 5, 6, 7, 8, 9, 10.
Class H: 1.

Class J: 1, 2, 3, 4, 5, 6, 7, 8, 9, 10, 11, 12, 13, 14, 15, 16, 17, 18, 19, 20, 21, 22, 23, 24, 25, 26, 27, 28, 31, 32, 33, 34, 35, 36, 37, 50, 51, 52, 53, 54, 55, 56, 57, 58, 59, 60, 61, 62, 63, 65, 66, 67, 68, 69, 70, 71, 72, 73, 74, 75, 76, 77, 78, 79, 80, 81, 82, 83, 84, 85, 86, 88, 90, 91.
Class K: 1, 2, 3.
Class L: 1.
Class M: 1.
Class N: 1, 2, 4, 5, 6, 7, 8, 9, 10, 11, 12, 13, 14, 15.
Class O: 1, 2, 4, 5.
Class Q: 1, 2, 3, 4, 5, 6, 7, 10.
Class R: 1.
Class S: 1.
Class T: 1.
Class X: 1, 2, 3, 4.
Class Y: 2, 4, 5, 6, 7, 8, 9, 10.
Class Z: 4, 5.

Additional classes were allocated from time to time as further but smaller railways were absorbed by the LNER. These included the Colne Valley & Halstead Railway, the East & West Yorkshire Union Railways, the Mid-Suffolk Light Railway, the Midland & Great Northern Joint Railway and the steam services of London Transport. Between them these railways added Classes F9, N19, J84, 85, 64, C17, D52, 53, 54, J40, 41, 93, M2, H2 and L2. Not all of the locomotives included in the above were of the same type in a class and seem to have been lumped together as a matter of convenience. During Gresley's tenure of office it was not usual to reuse numbers as they became vacant due to withdrawals. By April 1941, when Gresley died in office, a number of classes had been added by new building and rebuilding of existing designs. Class A4, B17, D49, J38, 39, K4, P1, U1, V1, V2, V3, V4, W1 and Y3 were new designs, while the new classes to emerge from substantial rebuildings were A3, A8 and C9.

Modifications and differences within each class also brought about a further sub-division of the basic class. For example Class P2 was a 2-8-2 express passenger design fitted with poppet valves. It was reclassified P2/1 in October 1934 to differentiate the original locomotives from those introduced the same date, but fitted with Walschaerts' valve gear and piston valves, which became P2/2. Some large classes had quite extensive sub-divisions, the Robinson-designed 0-8-0 goods engines going from Class 04/1 to 04/8.

Following Gresley's death the CME post was occupied by Edward Thompson and with his appointment many of the Gresley traditions were to disappear for a while or to undergo extensive modification. His tenure of office saw the addition of classes K5, Y11, J45, 06 and J94. He also reused classes A2, K1 and Q1 which had since become vacant.

A number of locomotives were to change their classes during the time of Gresley and Thompson but the latter was far more interested in standardization than his predecessor. To this end he was actively looking at a marked reduction not only in the variety of locomotive types but also in the way they were classified. Some idea of what might have happened can be gained by looking at the rebuild of a Class D49 'Hunt' which on its emergence from works as a two inside-cylindered locomotive was simply classified D. Similarly Thompson's numerically large class of B1 4-6-0 tender locomotives were originally allocated Class B. The conditions imposed by a world at war however made any progress in this direction difficult and, with the idea stalled, Thompson retired on 30 June 1946. His successor, Arthur H. Peppercorn, became CME with the LNER destined to last for only a further eighteen months. He added only one new class, 07, to the list but also designed two new classes of Pacific, neither of which were given new class numbers.

Finally, let's look at the classification of steam railcars. These were obtained from two manufacturers, Clayton and Sentinel-Cammell. The Clayton cars were classified A, B and C, and the Sentinel-Cammell cars D to H, Ha and J depending upon variations within the class.

Selected models

The LNER modeller has a tremendous choice of locomotives when it comes to running a layout. The choice of what is available over the counter is rather more limited, but not as restricted as might first appear. Careful rebuilding of ready to run items can provide more variety and a few examples are given here. Some of the ready to run models listed here are currently in production, but others can be found fairly easily on the second-hand market.

Basic models:

Hornby (Triang)

Class A1 4-6-2 Pacific	Class B17 0-6-0 Tender
Class A3 4-6-2 Pacific	Class D49 4-4-0 Tender
Class A4 4-6-2 Pacific	Class J52 0-6-0 Tank
Class B12 4-6-0 Tender	Class J83 0-6-0 Tank

All but the Class J83 are quite convincing models. The Class A4 comes in several varieties, with single or double chimney and with or without side valances.

Trix

Class A2 4-6-2 Pacific
Class A3 4-6-2 Pacific
Class A4 4-6-2 Pacific

The A3 and A4 are both nice models as is the A2, but as it was the very last of the line to appear under LNER ownership its use to the LNER modeller is limited.

Mainline

Class J72 0-6-0 Tank
Class N2 0-6-2 Tank

These are very nice models indeed and allow for some rebuilding. The J72 can have two types of safety valve whilst the N2 can run with or without condensing gear. Many of the latter ran in Scotland where they were also fitted with replacement chimneys and domes to suit the Scottish loading gauge.

Dapol

Class J94 0-6-0 Tank

Another very nice model representing a class of 74 locos purchased from the Ministry of Supply in 1946.

Wrenn (Hornby)

Class N2 0-6-2 Tank

Stanier 8F 2-8-0 Tender

The N2 goes way back in time to the days of three rail model railways but is also obtainable in a two rail version. Being die-cast it runs well, but is not nearly as accurate as the Mainline version. The Stanier 8F 2-8-0 is another old timer but a very good model for all that and converts into a Class 06 with the minimum of effort.

It will be noted that the ready to run range of models is split between the Pacifics and a few tank locomotives with only a small number of intermediate types in the middle. In addition to these ready to run models there are also a number of body-line kits made to fit onto an appropriate ready to run chassis. These include:

Wills

Class J39 0-6-0 Tender

Keyser

Class J50 0-6-0 Tank

Add to these the ever growing range of both white metal and brass kits, and the range is quite extensive. With the exception of the latter most of these kits are capable of being built by the moderately experienced modeller. The inexperienced modeller would do well to begin with the ready to run models and progress through the body-line kits to the more advanced work. Another way of both gaining experience and widening the scope of available models is to undertake a few conversion jobs.

'Nobody can make a good loco out of plastic card'. Really? This body is nearly ten years old and has spent the summer in the greenhouse, been left out on frosty nights, snowed upon and rained upon for weeks on end. It is as good as the day it was made.

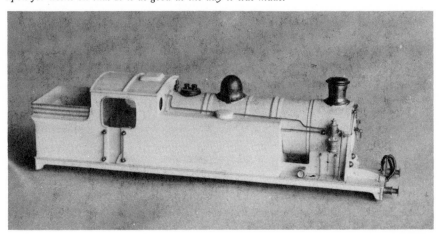

A simple conversion

To illustrate the methods that can be used a description is given of how to carry out a conversion which, with minor changes, produces not one but two versions of the same basic class. The subject is a Hornby (Triang) LNER Class B12 4-6-0 tender locomotive.

As supplied this model purports to be a Class B12/3, the Gresley rebuilt version of the original GER design with a small cab and larger diameter boiler. Comparison of the model with photographs will immediately show up one obvious discrepancy — the boiler does not look large enough in diameter and herein lies a trap for the unwary when reading drawings or tables of dimensions. The boiler diameter quoted is, more often than not, just that and does not include the layer of insulation and outer metal cladding. This can add an inch or two to the overall diameter, so beware. Perhaps this is what has happened to the B12/3. However all is not lost and it so happens that the boiler diameter is exactly correct for any of the earlier versions and for the later Thompson rebuild. The model also suffers from being too short. This can be rectified as all of the foreshortening has been done between the rear of the smokebox and the front of the leading splasher.

With any extensive rebuilding such as this one a decision needs to be made early on as to whether to use new or second-hand models. It takes a particular kind of courage, or stupidity, depending upon your viewpoint, to take a brand new model out of its box and then saw it up. It is up to you.

Conversion parts list
1 B12 locomotive complete
1 B12 locomotive body
1 chimney
1 dome

A Keyser white metal body kit designed to fit onto a Wrenn chassis. A good first step into metal model making, and a useful general purpose locomotive to boot.

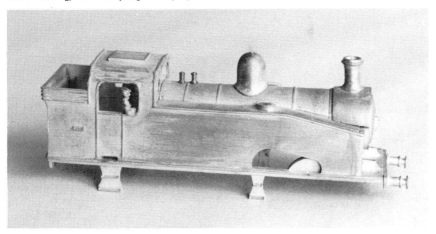

1 Westinghouse pump
4 vacuum pipes
Handrail knobs and wire
Plastic card of 10, 20 and 30 thou thicknesses
1 drawing and photographs

Remove the body from the chassis and remove the safety valves and whistle from the body. Holding the body on a small piece of wood, to protect the footsteps, cut away all of the original cab down to but not including the interior box splashers. From the old cab front mark the boiler 68 mm towards the smokebox end and saw through including the footplate and framing. Discard the smokebox end. Great care should be taken to ensure that all cutting is square and vertical. Mark the boiler at 5 mm and again at 35 mm from the old cab front. Saw through the body at the 5 mm mark down to, but not including, the footplate. At the 35 mm mark saw down to the level of the moulded handrails. This cutting operation weakens the body moulding considerably, so careful handling is called for. Carve or cut away all trace of the round-topped firebox down to handrail level between the saw cuts. Cut away the remains of the original moulded Westinghouse pump, clean up and fill as necessary.

Turning to the second body, mark off at 14.5 mm behind the smokebox and again saw right through including the footplate and framing. Retain the front portion, removing the smokebox door for later use. Now saw vertically through the front of the smokebox so that it is level with the front of the smokebox saddle. Remove the chimney, snifting valve and dome from their respective portions of the body. File or cut away all trace of the original boiler bands, but the reversing rod and moulded handrail can be left for the moment. Remove the hinge arms from the smokebox door, but not the hinge itself. This completes the major surgery and it is about now that you begin to ask yourself why you ever started in the first instance. From here on in it gets better.

The two body halves must now be joined together. Make sure that all is square and parallel — the moulded handrails, footplate and framing can be used to ensure correct lining up. Run a liquid cement such as Mekpak around the joints and set aside to dry. Cut a piece of 10 thou plastic card and bend to circular section in the fingers. This should be fitted up inside the model at the boiler joint to form a reinforcement and cemented in place. Check the body against the drawing and it should now be to scale length. Remove the BR number plate from the smokebox door and rub down with fine wet and dry. Using the drawing mark out on a piece of 10 thou plastic card the inside and outside diameters of the smokebox hinge ring. Using a pair of old dividers scribe out the outside diameter until cut through. Use the same method on the inside diameter to produce a ring. Remove a small piece to clear the top lamp bracket, place it on the smokebox door and fix with liquid cement. The door can now be fitted to the smokebox. Cut away all traces of the moulded handrails and rub down all round. Using 30 thou plastic card cut a rectangle to form the upper front portion of the Belpaire firebox and fix in position. From the same material cut two sides and a top and similarly fix in position so that the top is flush with and parallel to the boiler top. The new firebox will now look like an inverted box. After all joints have set hard build up the inside of the box with 30 thou card sufficient to allow the top corners and edges to be rounded off. It is important to round off these top corners with care as the final profile forms the lower edge of the cab front windows. Cut the cab front from 30 thou plastic card wide enough so that it takes up the full cab width and the new sides can be butted up to it. Mark and cut out the spectacle windows. Mark out two cab sides and cut to shape. These will fit on top of the box splashers and butt against the front. A good fit can be obtained by trial and error. Fit the beading to the cab windows before fixing the cab sides to the body. A roof support arch should now be cut and fixed behind the second set of cab side windows. Use a straight edge to test that the height of the arch is such that the roof, when fitted, will be parallel with the boiler top. Fit cab glazing if desired.

Cut a piece of 20 thou plastic card to form the roof. Lightly score one side along its length and it will begin to curve. Ease to the correct contour with the fingers and fix in place. When rubbed down the score lines will disappear and the rain strips can then be added.

At this stage leave everything to set hard and go back to studying the photographs. Although large numbers of locos might all nominally belong to the same class and have been built by one builder they could, and often did, acquire detailed differences during subsequent visits to works. On this particular batch of B12s the one noticeable difference between them concerns the shape of the blower pipe mounted high up on the boiler on the locomotive's right hand side. Photographs show clearly that it appears at the top corner of the firebox and enters the smokebox in the same position on all locomotives. It is what happens in between that matters. Some pipes run parallel with the boiler and are kinked down at the smokebox end, at least one slopes downwards in a straight line, whilst the one on the locomotive illustrated kinks downwards just forward of the dome. These details matter and make for models with character.

Boiler fittings, boiler banding, new footsteps and other detail work can now be added. Cut away the cab front inside the boiler sufficiently to clear the motor. The whole can now be given a coat of grey paint and examined for flaws before being sent to the paint shop.

The chassis requires only three modifications, all of them simple. Driving wheel balance weights were very prominent on the B12 so that new ones need to be cut out from 10 thou plastic card and fixed over the top of the existing ones. As the body is now longer a new link will have to be made for the leading bogie if it is to fit under the body in the correct position. Finally take off the coupling rods and swap side for side so that the joint is ahead of the centre crank pin. Reference to the photograph will clearly show where most of the work has been undertaken, as the modifications have been painted white for clarity.

This description is designed to illustrate how even the most common of models can be improved and provide the modeller with a greater variety. Using exactly the same conversion methods, with the exception of the firebox, another version of

Above *LNER Class A4 No 24* Kingfisher *in post-war livery with post-1946 numbering. It is fitted with 'stainless steel' numbers and letters. This is a modified and repainted Hornby model.*

Top left *Originally a Triang model of LNER Class B12/3, this model has been rebuilt backwards in time to represent a B12 in near original condition. With large cab and Belpaire firebox, the modifications are shown in white. The boiler has also been extended to scale length.*

Middle left *Similarly rebuilt to the Class B12 with the Belpaire firebox, this version has a round-topped firebox and was classified as B12/25A, indicating the fitting of a diagram 25A boiler. Note the difference style of blower pipe and altered position of the Westinghouse brake pump compared with other B12s.*

Bottom left *A complete view of the Class B12/25A. Note the unlined black livery, small lettering on the tender and twin brake hoses.*

Below *A stranger indeed. Built at Darlington in August 1946 to a Stanier design of the LMS, 3144 was part of the 68-strong LNER Class 06. Renumbered 8749, it returned to its rightful owners in October 1947. Versions of the same loco built at Doncaster had disc tender wheels. This example is a Wrenn model.*

the same class can be created. This is the Thompson rebuild which retained a round-topped firebox when equipped with a diagram 25A boiler. These locomotives became Class B12/4 under BR ownership.

It is not too difficult to find other models which will repay a few hours' work in this way. The Mainline Class N2 is already mentioned. Two conversions based upon 'Flying Scotsman' are illustrated, whilst the Class A4 only needs a replacement chimney to open up the whole class — a point, incidentally, neatly ignored by some manufacturers when they reintroduce the same model in a different livery. Under LNER ownership only four of the streamliners were fitted with double chimneys, the rest being converted by BR.

Some conversions, such as that illustrated by the Class 06 (Stanier 8F), are accomplished by the paint brush and are quick and easy to do. Various kits can be modified and are in some ways easier as with a little thought the conversion can be accomplished either before or during building. Such is the J39 to J38 conversion using a Wills kit, also illustrated. In short, although the ready to run market has never been over-generous in the provision of LNER motive power, the picture is not quite as bleak as might at first appear. Besides, there is much more satisfaction to be gained from running something that has an element of skill in its construction than running something straight out of the box.

Two from one. A Wills Class J39 at the top and a modified version, Class J38, below. The J38 has smaller driving wheels and no splashers.

Above *A close-up view of the Class J38. The modifications to the footplate are clearly visible.*

Below *The Class J38 ready for the road. Although the Class J39 was widely distributed throughout the LNER, this class was confined to Scotland, mainly in and around the Fife coalfields.*

Chapter 3

Passenger rolling stock

At its inception in 1923 the LNER inherited a variety of coaching stock both mainline and suburban. Some of this was of considerable vintage with a noticeable disparity in lengths, heights and roof profiles. Reference to photographs taken at the time will show that the roof line of many trains was quite uneven. It is also apparent that the prototype got away with train formations that do not always work in model form. It is not unusual to see a small six-wheeled vehicle marshalled between the locomotive and a heavy train of bogie stock.

All of the constituent mainline companies had built their own coaches in their own works. The GNR established its main works for locomotive and rolling stock construction at Doncaster in 1853, although it was not until 1857 that this works began producing coaches. The NER set up its carriage works in 1867 at York, the NBR had its works at Cowlairs and the GNoSR at Inverurie. The GER built its coaches at Stratford and the GCR had it works at Dukinfield.

In general terms all of these railways had evolved carriage design along similar lines with four-wheeled stock giving way to six-wheeled stock. Bogie stock on both eight and sometimes twelve wheels followed, some companies going through an intermediate stage of rigid eight-wheeled stock. Wooden-bodied coaches of the most rudimentary design, mounted on wooden underframes and lit by gas were to evolve into wooden-bodied coaches on steel underframes lit by electricity. One reason for the change was the unfortunate tendency for all wooden vehicles to telescope in a collision, and being gas lit this could and often did lead to a fire. As designs changed, so too did building materials and all-steel coaches had been built prior to 1923 including some massive all-steel dining cars for the NBR. Around this time too the rather sparse style of interior decoration and fitments had given way, on mainline stock, to heavily ornate fittings in the grand Victorian manner.

Similar in evolution though the various companies, coaches were, they none the less adopted their own variations in style so that it is often possible to identify the parent company by such characteristics as roof curvature and details of panelling. Parallel to this there was already evolving a pattern of vehicle that approached a standard design although again detailed differences were apparent. These vehicles were used for the East Coast Joint Services, being built and financed jointly by the GNR at Doncaster, the NER at York and the NBR at Cowlairs. In spite of a steady attempt by the NER to influence design features from York it appears that the GNR was the dominant partner. The appointment of H. N. Gresley, the former Carriage and Wagon Superintendent to the GNR, as Chief Mechanical

Photographed at York in August 1965, full brake E70524E shows well the arrangement of panelling and beading on Gresley coaches.

Engineer to the LNER, no doubt helped to ensure that the GNR influence was carried over into LNER design thinking.

In fairness it is a matter of record that the GNR had pioneered the way in coach design in many areas. The first bogie vehicle was built in 1874 and two years later the now familiar three centre round roof was adopted. The GNR pioneered the very first British restaurant car in 1879 and followed this up with the first British side corridor coach. Similarly, the standard design features already evident on the ECJS stock, such as the three centre round roof with sloping ends and curved coach sides, was to influence and set the standard for all LNER coach design as long as Gresley remained in office. Externally the GNR coach tended to be rather severe with square corners to panelling and windows. NER stock was not unlike GNR stock in outline and both possessed bow-ended eliptical roofed stock. However, panelling and window corners on NER stock were formed with a small radius making this feature less harsh. Matchboard panelling was also used below waist level for a time before a return to the more orthodox style. Some NER designs continued in production until 1925, examples being supplied to the Southern Scottish Area and others to the former lines of the GER.

The GNoSR had built coaches right up until the grouping. This was panelled stock with rounded corners. Roofs were quite flat in profile and top lights were a feature of their coaches. All coach building at Inverurie ceased soon after the grouping. Between the end of the First World War and grouping the NBR did little in the way of coach design. It too had produced panelled coaches with the corners to both panelling and windows rounded off. Roofs were again to a flattish profile. The GER too had used a distinctive body panelling style. Below a quite broad waist panel the lower panels were divided by vertical beading. Coach work at Stratford ceased at the grouping and was not resumed until 1927. The GCR vehicles were often quite massive in appearance with matchboard sides. This matchboarding finished at waist level on some vehicles and continued to roof height on others. The general use of panelling apart, the products of the NBR, GNoSR, GER and GCR did little to influence what were to become standard design features of LNER coaching stock. However many of these pre-grouping vehicles were to have long lives in LNER ownership. As new or replacement stock became available it was often the custom to 'cascade' coaches to lesser lines or duties. Even after this some coaches found themselves cascaded even further to become camping coaches, stores, tool and mess vans for permanent way or breakdown gangs. Thus it was occasionally possible to see vehicles of pre-grouping design that had long outlived the LNER. Similarly, a number of LNER vehicles could still be seen well into the BR era.

LNER coaches from two manufacturers. The rear vehicle is from Hornby and is shorter than scale. This shows up against the full brake to exact scale length from Ian Kirk.

Much has been written elsewhere and at great length about the coaching stock designed under Gresley and it is not intended to try and provide a potted history here of all the general and special designs. For the purposes of the railway modeller, and bearing in mind the availability of coach kits and ready to run models, it is perhaps more convenient to break down the stock types in a different fashion. The basic division is by three, being suburban non-corridor, mainline corridor and special stock. The latter includes set trains such as the 'Flying Scotsman', 'Silver Jubilee', 'Coronation' and tourist stock. The problem with nearly all LNER passenger stock as far as the modeller is concerned can be summed up in one word used many times in this chapter — panelling.

Not the easiest thing to make, any panelled coach is going to test the patience, dexterity and probably the eyesight of the modeller. Trade offerings until comparatively recently have been few, the aluminium or brass kit being relatively easy to assemble but requiring a lot of detail work to complete. The three ready to run vehicles, a sleeper first, composite and brake composite offered by Hornby, were commendable efforts in their way but suffered from the usual concessions made necessary by the market at which they were aimed and the restrictions of mass production. None the less the representation of the panel work and beading is very well done. As described elsewhere in this book, given a few modifications and a repaint they can be converted into nice models.

If ever a model was ripe for production as an injection moulded kit then the LNER coach was it. Fortunately this has now been recognized, with several manufacturers responding with limited offerings. The most comprehensive range currently on offer comes from Ian Kirk, Model Engineering, of Fife. The range of 51 ft $1\frac{1}{2}$ in non-corridor stock is comprised of a sufficient number of vehicles to produce a train typical of the lesser LNER lines or one that would have been seen on the cross-country lines. A similar range of 61 ft mainline corridor stock is available so that a typical express train can be constructed. The prototypes have been chosen with some care so that it now possible to construct a complete 'Flying Scotsman' train including the characteristic articulated triplet restaurant set. Articulated stock is also available in the suburban range, an example of which is illustrated here.

Articulation of coaches was a feature to be found amongst LNER coaching stock, in this case a third/third twin. Although it made for lighter trains it could be a problem as a fault on one coach took both out of service. This example was made from an Ian Kirk kit.

As with locomotives, a little research can reveal ways of extending the basic range. For example, the 51 ft 1½ in suburban seven compartment all-first can also be used as a composite or an all-third. A number were reclassified to make up for a shortage of this type of stock. In similar fashion the four-compartment brake third can be converted into a push-pull unit. A conversion in model form is simple and increases the basic range.

Above *A part completed 51 ft 1½ in non-corridor brake third from an Ian Kirk kit, modified to a push-pull coach. Note the extra window at the driving end.*

Left *End view of the driving portion of the push-pull coach. The end windows on this version are much larger than on the standard brake third.*

The method of building Kirk kits is basically the same whether the kit is for a corridor or non-corridor vehicle. The modeller used to building plastic kits of ships or aircraft will notice one difference with Kirk kits — very few locating pips or lugs are moulded on so that lining up, say the sides with the ends, can be a little problematical until the trick is learned. Reference to a drawing will show that the top of the side fits on the same line as the cross conduit moulded on the end. With this part assembled accurately all the rest will fall into place. This does not arise on the corridor stock as it is obvious where the side and end mouldings meet. There is one other area where care needs to be taken even before assembly commences. The injection moulding process puts quite a thick sprue above the cant rail. On the corridor stock in particular it is all too easy to let enthusiasm overrule common sense and be tempted to break this away. This action puts a tremendous load onto the moulding at its weakest point. It is more than likely that the side will break away at the window apertures. A little bit of applied patience and a razor saw will solve this problem. With all the parts separated and thoroughly cleaned up construction can commence. Study the instruction sheet and any good photographs before beginning. Before using any adhesive always try the fit of parts with a dry run. It has not been unknown for an instruction sheet to be wrong (not in these particular kits), and at least one coach kit, not LNER, cannot be assembled in the manner indicated, a fact that only becomes apparent when it is too late.

The reason is not known, but experience has shown that Mekpak is not the best adhesive to use when fixing the glazing on these kits. It is better to use Daywat which seems to give a much stronger bond between these two materials. More than one coach has had to return to 'works' after the glazing became detached — not a complete disaster, but a nuisance. Mekpak is however perfectly satisfactory to assemble the rest of the kit.

To illustrate construction methods let us consider a brake third corridor kit. The basic body kit consists of two ends, a two piece floor, the sides in four pieces and a roof moulding. The sides are moulded in this way to allow for easy construction of the crank in the body side marking the division between the passenger and brake sections. A boss is moulded onto the underside of the floor mouldings on which to mount the bogies. Make sure that these are at the outer ends when assembly begins, this may sound obvious, but such a silly mistake can easily be made.

Some jobs will need to be done prior to the main assembly. These are the fixing of the glazing and corridor handrails, painting the toilet windows white and fixing the bogie mounting screws. Drill out the holes in the floor mouldings to take the bogie fixing screws using a 5/64ths drill. (This is an extremely useful size of drill to have as it also does for drilling the bogie side frames to accept 'top hat' bearings and for drilling the roof to accept white metal torpedo ventilators if the ones in the kit are not used.) The brass screws can now be screwed in from the top and, as they are a tight fit, require no other form of fixing. Note that the body end mouldings are of slightly different widths. This is to allow for the fact already mentioned that the body is narrower over the brake portion. Having identified the correct end, mark it with a letter B in soft pencil on its inside face.

Before fixing the glazing, paint all the door and window apertures, including those in the corridor partition, with teak paint. On the brake end the top lights go almost to the end of the body side so that the glazing should be carefully trimmed to allow room for the coach end to butt up properly. Make up the corridor handrails from fine brass wire and fix to the glazing with a small blob of fast-setting epoxy resin adhesive. A cocktail stick is an ideal tool for this task, enabling small amounts of adhesive to be placed exactly where they are needed. Paint toilet windows white on the inside and set aside to dry.

At this stage it is a good idea to make a decision on what type of underframe truss rodding is to be fitted. The LNER continued to use the GNR type of turnbuckle arrangement up until 1930 on this type of vehicle. Thereafter the underframe truss was made of angle iron. This is one of those areas where strict adherence to scale modelling may not be the most practical solution. Whilst the parts supplied to make up the angle iron version are perfectly adequate, a turnbuckle arrangement made out of plastic rod is a somewhat spidery affair. One excursion off the track could well take the underframe with it. To solve this problem make up the posts from small split pins set into suitably drilled holes in the solebars. The rodding should be made up from steel wire, passed through the pins and glued to the inside edge of the solebars. This is a far stronger job and will easily cope with the odd unscheduled excursion into the six foot.

The underside of the floor moulding carries a representation of the coach framing and has location pips for the solebars. Before fitting these it is wise to consider the smallest radius curve you will require the vehicle to negotiate as, if it is too restricted, the wheels will inhibit sufficient bogie swing. It is possible to ease the solebars out a little in width without spoiling the look of the model, the extra width gained between them allowing for greater bogie swing. If it is intended to construct a number of coaches it is a good idea to make a distance gauge out of plastic or brass so that all vehicles will be constructed to the same standard. This illustrates another point to be borne in mind when doing any modelling — always try to plan two or three moves ahead as it will save time and trouble in the long run. As another example, the kit contains two special cranked mouldings which are used to join the two halves of the side together and establish the correct relative inset distance. It does not require a BSc to work out what they are for or how they fit but care in positioning is called for so that they do not impede the fitting of the floor or glazing. Assembly of the kit can now continue, taking great care not to get any adhesive onto the glazing. With the basic body assembled attention can now be turned to the interior. This is best made up on the work bench and fitted as a complete unit. Before fitting the roof be sure to check that everything inside is well and truly stuck down. As a matter of production expediency some of the smaller frets provided with these kits contain more parts than are actually needed. Do not assume that it all has to go somewhere. Enough battery box parts are supplied to make up four boxes but only two should be fitted.

By and large the manufacturers produce sufficient vehicles to satisfy those who wish to run everyday trains. For the modeller wishing to run the more exotic stock such as that used on the 'Silver Jubilee' or 'Coronation' then the answer for the

Designed in 1944, the deal-boarded full brake makes an ideal first exercise in coach scratch building as it is straight sided. Awaiting lettering, the model is not quite what it seems as none of the windows is actually there. They were painted on after construction, including shadow lines to give the illusion of depth.

moment has to be scratch building. This can sound fairly daunting and sometimes not without justification. Have you ever really *looked* at the 'Coronation' beaver-tail observation car?

Scratch coach building need not be all that difficult however. Illustrated is a Thompson deal-boarded full brake which is in many ways an ideal subject for a first effort, having all the features of a coach but without the need to form the tumble home as they were straight sided.

The model is basically a plastic box fitted with a stripped off and redetailed second-hand coach roof. Construction is simple, being a case of transferring measurements off a drawing onto plastic card and then cutting out accurately. The doors and deal-board lines are then carefully scribed on and the whole assembled as any other plastic kit. There is still of course a trap for the unwary, which applies equally if the vehicle is a goods van. Supposing that the marking out and cutting has been done with extreme accuracy and the whole thing has been assembled absolutely square. It is possible to build an airtight box which will then respond to changes in the temperature or atmospheric pressure. This response will be visible as the sides bow in or bow out. If there appears to be a risk of this then drill a couple of small ventilation holes in the underside to allow the body to breathe. Alternatively the addition of a dial and a few levers could produce an unusual type of barometer for your hall. It would certainly be a talking point!

If you have ventured into coach building and the thought of all that panelling and beading is still daunting, what are the alternatives? The all-steel stock of the Gresley era is a possibility but remember that all casings and mouldings were painted on, so that may not solve the problem. From 1945 onwards the LNER built a number of all-steel coaches both corridor and non-corridor. These carried a simulated teak graining but were devoid of panelling, real or simulated, and were unlined. They were a radical departure from what had gone before but offer certain advantages to the modeller.

Edward Thompson, as CME, designed these corridor coaches at the instigation of Sir Charles Newton following a fatal fire on a north-bound train at Claypole. It was thought that the fatalities might have been avoided if cross-corridors had been available instead of doors at each end only. The new design meant that only one other compartment had to be passed before reaching a cross-corridor and external door. This arrangement also hastened the loading and unloading of passengers thus reducing station stop times and easing internal congestion.

By 1944, when the design was first considered, all timbers were in short supply so that steel panels on a timber frame was an attractive alternative. Externally all coaches were flush sided and to continue the company livery they were finished in an artificial teak graining. Roofs were now straight at the ends, made of canvas-covered timber and painted white, although they quickly became grey in service. Coaches were built from 1945 onwards and there were two distinct varieties. Those intended for use on the 'Flying Scotsman' and 'Junior Scotsman' sets were double glazed and had pressure ventilation with Air-Vac roof ventilators mounted near the coach ends. The body side came down level with the lower edge of the solebar and cut-outs were provided at the steps. Windows had square corners on LNER-built vehicles although subsequent problems with corrosion forced a change to rounded corners after 1949. Compartments had wood veneer panelling.

Similar vehicles built for general service stock were not double glazed and had ordinary torpedo ventilators on the roof. Body side panels finished in the more usual fashion at the top edge of the solebars. Compartments had cream paintwork. All underframes were of angle iron and buffers were round with clipped tops. Each compartment was serviced by two torpedo ventilators mounted twelve inches off the roof centre-line towards the compartment side. Those over brake compartments were on the roof centre-line. Ventilators over toilet compartments varied in their location depending upon the type of vehicle. On full firsts and full thirds they were on the roof centre-line but on some brake ended vehicles they were offset to match the compartment ventilators. Only the doors to first class portions of vehicles carried a brand. Compartment sizes were standardized, 7 ft 6 in for first class and 6 ft 6 in for third class.

The non-corridor stock of all-steel construction was very similar in outline and internal layout to the Gresley stock that went before. Vehicles to these two designs continued to be built after nationalization in 1948 and some of the corridor stock and non-passenger coaching stock lasted long enough to be repainted in rail blue and the blue/grey scheme.

Chapter 4

Non-passenger coaching stock and self-propelled stock

As well as vehicles designed to carry passengers, the LNER inherited or introduced non-passenger carrying vehicles that were none the less classified as coaching stock. They often ran as part of a passenger train formation but could equally well form complete trains in their own right. Designed for the carriage of mail, parcels, light goods, pigeon traffic and even bread, some types were a common sight all over the system. As with passenger carrying stock two basic types existed. The first of these shared the same underframe and general construction details as the 61 ft passenger stock, including the three arc roof profile with elliptical ends. Initially the carrying capacity was 8 tons and was carried on GNR or LNER bogies of 8 ft wheelbase. Later this was increased to 10 tons and many were mounted on standard LNER bogies of 8 ft 6 in wheelbase.

Several variations on the basic theme were built, including a batch of all-steel vehicles built in 1927. Some batches of vehicles carried guards duckets whilst others were devoid of this feature. On some, shelving was provided throughout and these were used for the conveyance of racing pigeons, a sport very popular in certain areas through which the LNER operated. The general design continued to be built throughout the LNER's existence both in teak and steel construction. Towards the end of the war new vehicles were built, but because teak was virtually unobtainable these had horizontal deal boarding for both sides and ends. Later still an all-steel version appeared and both these and the deal version were built to the general outline adopted for the Newton/Thompson design.

Vehicles were also introduced to the shorter non-vestibuled design of 51 ft 6 in stock. Again they shared the same general design features as their passenger carrying counterparts and served the same purpose as their larger brothers. Vehicles of both lengths are represented in the Ian Kirk range and by careful reference to drawings and photographs it is possible to ring the changes and build different varieties from the basic kit.

Taking the 61 ft 6 in version first it is possible to build an early version with truss rod underframe and a later version with angle iron underframing as well as versions with or without guards duckets. An interesting and unusual conversion concerns two vehicles that were converted to cinema cars in 1935 and 1936 respectively. Numbered 4040 and 4041 they had modified roof ventilators and carried the legend LNER PATHE CINEMA CAR on roof mounted boards. Internally they were decorated in typical cinema style of the period and films were shown using back projection. They ran in this manner until late in 1939 when

Above *An interesting and unusual variation on a theme. A standard full brake behind, and in front one of two similar vehicles converted for use as a cinema car. No 4040 was introduced in May 1935 and worked daily between London and Leeds. A second conversion, No 4041 was introduced in March 1936 for the Leeds-Glasgow-Edinburgh service. Coach roof boards were red with white lettering. Both coaches reverted to full brakes in 1939.*

Below *Another view of the 61 ft 6 in full brake made from an Ian Kirk kit. This type of van often travelled far off the parent system, especially when carrying racing pigeons.*

Above *An Ian Kirk kit provided this non-vestibuled bogie brake van, built as a later version with guard's ducket and angle iron underframe.*

Below *Non-vestibuled bogie brake van, the same length and profile as non-gangwayed surburban stock. Not fitted with a ducket, it does have the earlier type of truss rod underframe. This was built from an Ian Kirk kit.*

both were converted again to ordinary full brake vehicles.

The 51 ft 6 in stock also provides variety for the modeller by similar variations in ducket and underframe details. On a small layout a short rake of these vehicles would be ideal for delivering the morning papers or collecting the milk.

Another interesting vehicle not often seen in model form is the Travelling Post Office. This is probably because few modellers have the space to operate such vehicles in anything approaching prototypical practice. Operated by the railway, the cost of new TPO construction was paid for jointly by the Post Office and the railway company concerned. At grouping the LNER inherited TPO vehicles from the GNR, NER and GER. Many of these were of considerable vintage, being clerestory roofed and gas lit. In 1929, following considerable pressure from the Post Office, new vehicles to an LNER design were introduced. Obviously, as highly specialized vehicles they had a shape that was dictated by their purpose but followed the standard designs in general finish, being teak panelled and fully lined out.

In addition to the bogie stock outlined above there were also a number of long wheelbase four-wheeled vans. These were again of two types. The first had matchboard sides and were fitted internally for milk or pigeon traffic. The second type were also equipped in some cases for pigeon traffic but the rest were general service vehicles. This type had teak panelled bodies and were similar in finish to other teak stock.

Self–propelled stock

The LNER inherited a system where steam haulage predominated but there were two electrified lines. The first was on North Tyneside and was a passenger carrying line with third rail electrification. The second line was to the west of Middlesbrough, used for coal and mineral traffic, and was electrified by overhead wire. In addition, by 1931, the LNER had co-operated with the LMS in electrifying the Manchester, South Junction & Altrincham Railway, also with an overhead wire system. Several grand plans were drawn up during the existence of the LNER, including a scheme of co-operative development with the LPTB and the electrification of the trans-Pennine line between Manchester and Sheffield via Woodhead. In the event only part of the former was completed, development of the remainder being brought to an abrupt halt by the outbreak of World War 2. Completion of these and other schemes had to wait until after the LNER had lost its separate identity in nationalization.

NER Tyneside electric stock was in need of refurbishment and replacement and at a review of rolling stock undertaken in 1934 authorization was given for the construction of new vehicles. The eventual total was 164 multiple-unit coaches made up into twins. These were then formed into trains of various lengths as traffic demanded. The vehicles were of all-steel construction, open inside but divided into two saloons. Large windows were fitted together with large sliding ventilators, one to each window. Manually operated doors were provided at the ends of each coach.

By the mid-1920s the railways were beginning to suffer badly on certain lines

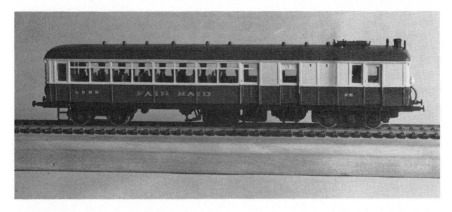

Boyhood memories — a Sentinel-Cammell steam railcar in which I travelled as a child. A white metal kit by Nu-Cast. Numbered in the coaching series but kept in loco sheds, the real thing was not always as clean at this one, inside or out.

from the competition being offered by the private motor car and the motor bus. In a bid to remain competitive the LNER, in company with many other railways, began to look around for ways to counter this growing threat and to effect economies in operation. The well tried and traditional branch line train was not the most economic means of transporting passengers and so in 1925 the LNER was to embark on the introduction of the steam railcar. At first these were operated in very small numbers until by 1927 a batch of eleven was obtained from the Clayton Wagon Co to assess their operation against the cars already in service from the Sentinel-Cammell. All were operated in the north-eastern area and were somewhat curious vehicles with their power bogie having coupled wheels and their coal supply carried in a small bunker at one end.

All of the railcars of either design were to suffer from the same operating defect. This was their inability to cope with peak demands such as those made on market days for example. In an attempt to alleviate this problem the LNER also purchased from Clayton a number of trailer cars which provided additional capacity. When first introduced they were finished in simulated teak or plum and cream but from 1930 onwards all were to carry the standard scheme of engine green below the waist and cream above. They outlasted the Clayton steam railcars and were then paired with Sentinel-Cammell cars. All had gone by 1940. These trailers brought about an operating problem of their own as at the end of the line the powered car had to be run round the trailer, there being no provision for driving.

A total of 81 Sentinel-Cammell steam railcars were purchased between 1925 and 1932. There were design differences within this total including rigid bodied cars, articulated cars and one articulated twin. All but three were named, these names being those formerly used on stage coaches and each car carried within it a notice offering a small monetary reward for additional information on the original coach.

Although at first glance the Sentinel-Cammell steam railcar appears to be easy to model, closer inspection will reveal that it is not as simple as it first appears. With recessed doors, thin window pillars and its fair share of louvres there is more than enough detail work. To the operator of a small branch type of layout however it is still attractive as it offers a compact unit. Fortunately Nu-Cast have produced an excellent white metal kit of the Type H rigid bodied car of which there were fifty. A model of number 32, *Fair Maid*, is illustrated here and was built from one of these kits. It is a very heavy model and is quite prototypical in that it does not take too kindly to having too many additional vehicles added to it. None the less it could cope with a lightweight model of one of the Clayton trailer cars. This combination will also provide a bright splash of colour on a branch layout which is not usually the haunt of green or blue locomotives. The Sentinel-Cammell cars outlasted the Clayton cars by some eight years. The majority were withdrawn from 1943 onwards with the final car being withdrawn in February 1948. This event was not without a touch of irony as the car carried the name *Hope*.

Other traction

Although steam was the predominant prime mover, from time to time the various railways took a long hard look at alternative methods. These could be particularly attractive on those lines where the service, although socially desirable, offered a very low return on operating cost. The Southern Railway operated electric traction to a greater extent than any of the others in the Big Four. The Great Western Railway successfully operated a fleet of diesel railcars, whilst the London, Midland & Scottish Railway had ventured, late in its existence, into express passenger haulage with diesel locomotives 10000 and 10001.

Of the LNER constituents the NER had pioneered the way in a limited fashion. Prior to its absorption it had built a prototype express electric locomotive. However, a few trial runs apart, it was destined never to earn its keep. The intention had been to electrify the east coast main line between York and Newcastle but this scheme was never implemented. The locomotive itself existed for the life of the LNER being scrapped in 1949. In 1928 the LNER was to investigate the use of heavy haulage by diesel traction but again nothing was to become of this exercise. Another investigation was carried out in 1947 along similar lines as although the company operated a large fleet of steam locomotives they were by this time to old designs and new designs were needed. Again this scheme was shelved, not only because the LNER ceased to exist, but because of the decision taken early by British Railways to introduce their own standard designs of steam locomotives.

Not all plans came to nothing, however. In the early 1930s a 250 hp oil-electric railcar was purchased, having previously run trials in the North-east. Built by W.G. Armstrong-Whitworth Co it must have impressed somebody because in April 1934 two more were purchased from the same source. Attractively painted in blue and cream livery, they all had trailer cars and were also named, as follows: 25 *Tyneside Venturer*, 224 *Lady Hamilton*, and 232 *Northumbrian*. Unfortunately their serviceability rate failed to live up to expectation and a decision was reached in 1939 that they were beyond economic repair and so they were withdrawn. In 1934 and also from Armstrong-Whitworth the LNER purchased a 60 seat diesel-electric railbus. Although the experiments might have continued and the introduction of mainline diesel or electric traction might have been implemented on a grand scale, the outbreak of war in 1939 effectively ended any further development in this area.

The LNER also investigated shunting locomotives at an early stage. Another Armstrong-Whitworth design of six coupled locomotive was investigated in 1932 but this too seems to have failed to produce any conclusive results. It was to be 1947 before the matter was raised again and in that year the LNER was successfully operating four diesel shunters in its Whitemoor Yard.

Mention has already been made of the proposal to electrify the trans-Pennine line between Manchester and Sheffield via Woodhead and in 1941 the first locomotive appeared numbered 6701. This was the prototype of Class EM1 which later became BR Class 76. Shortly after the end of the war this locomotive was loaned to the Netherlands Railway to assist in the post-war recovery of their system. Subsequently returning to Britain it was named *Tommy* and then employed on its intended duties, the electrification scheme having finally been completed in 1954.

From the viewpoint of the LNER modeller, the use of most of the aforementioned types is strictly limited both in area and period of operation. Additionally, there are no kits available save for that of the Sentinel-Cammell steam railcar. However, they would certainly make interesting and different modelling projects. No detailed study has been undertaken, but the LNER design of diesel shunter is very similar in outline to the standard BR version so that it might be possible to carry out a conversion here provided that the main dimensions are not too far out.

Chapter 5

Freight stock

On 1 January 1923 the LNER became the owners of 284,488 freight vehicles (including brake vans) together with an additional 15,966 vehicles in service stock, or over 300,000 in all. Thus the LNER modeller is faced with a huge choice of possible prototypes, way beyond that which any model railway in the wildest imaginings could support. The intention then must be to select the more common types to give the overall feeling of LNER predominance. No doubt excuses could be dreamed up for running examples of the more exotic types but these would be an exception in everyday traffic. What then to model?

A study of statistics between the years 1929 and 1947 will reveal a definite trend in a number of areas of freight operation being reflected in the vehicle construction programme. Although the various constituent companies had all provided the same general service to their customers, the vehicles with which this was done varied both in construction and age. The LNER then set about introducing its own range of vehicles both to replace ageing stock and to provide additional capacity. This does not mean that pre-grouping designs were swept away and over 50,000 were still in traffic when the LNER ceased to exist. To indicate the general types of vehicles needed by the modeller the following figures give a good guide.

Open goods wagons (12 tons capacity)
In 1929 just over 58,000 were in service, rising to over 78,000 by 1947.

Little and large — 4 mm and 7 mm scale models of the same 45 ton 'Quad'. The smaller model is constructed from a plastic kit, the larger from a white metal kit with real timber decking. The letter 'N' at the end of the headstocks indicates that it is not a common user vehicle.

Covered goods vans (12 tons capacity)
In 1929 over 13,000 were in service, rising to over 40,000 by 1947.
Mineral wagons (12 tons capacity)
In 1929 almost 22,000 were in service, rising to over 31,000 by 1947.
Cattle trucks
In 1929 over 7,000 were in service but their numbers fell steadily off with the decline in this type of traffic until by 1947 the number was down to just over 2,500.
Brake vans
The introduction of standard designs and the phasing out of brake vehicles below 15 tons weight saw the 1929 figure of just over 2,500 reduced to 700 by 1947. To counterbalance this the number of brake vans of 20 tons weight and over had risen from just over 2,000 in 1929 to just under 4,000 in 1947.

It is easy to see then that any model railway layout that purports to represent the LNER will have a fair number of open wagons, covered goods vans and the necessary brake vans. Cattle trucks may also be in evidence but perhaps not in the quantity sometimes displayed. Within the broad headings of vehicle types were further sub-divisions, some of which were again more common than others. For example open goods wagons came with different numbers of planks in their sides, the six and seven plank version being common. Similarly, covered vans could be planked vertically or horizontally and have cupboard type or sliding doors. If the number of freight vehicles to be used on a layout is small then certainly some of the following should be represented.

Open goods wagons
The open goods wagon with full length dropsides was contributed in some numbers by every one of the constituent companies. These were of the two, three, or four plank variety. For this reason the LNER found no need to build any wagons of this type to its own designs. In addition, several of the pre-grouping companies operated fixed-sided open wagons, These were usually only one plank high but there were also two or three plank examples.

A pair of open wagons, the left hand one owes its origins to the GNoSR. The Boplate is typical of a type of bogie wagon built for a specific purpose, namely the carrying of steel plate.

Three styles of van. The right-hand vehicle is a vacuum fitted plywood LNER van showing the late style of lettering. The centre vehicle is a very early design of planked sliding door van in early livery. The left hand ex-NBR van is almost at the end of its useful life, but showing repairs to its planking in the recent past.

The pre-grouping design of open wagon to be found most often was fitted with doors in the middle of each side. These doors were hinged along their lower edge and, when lowered, allowed for easy loading and unloading against a platform or goods wharf. Capacity varied between 8 tons and 12 tons. Most were built on wooden underframes but some steel underframed examples existed in some numbers. Very many too had grease-filled axleboxes whilst braking arrangements could differ considerably. Some had single acting shoes, one to each side, while others had cross-connected brake levers with shoes acting against all wheels.

The first LNER standard design of open wagon was actually a GNR design, one hundred being constructed prior to grouping. These were built on a wooden underframe of 9 ft wheelbase. A small number of wagons to the same general design were also built with automatic vacuum brake gear. The 9 ft wheelbase open wagon continued to be built in considerable numbers until 1932 and from this date the wheelbase was increased to 10 ft. Production continued and in the mid-1940s the underframes were made of steel. A further but much larger batch of automatic vacuum braked wagons to this design was built in the latter half of the 1930s. By 1938 the number of planks on this type of wagon had been reduced to five. Although timber was the main construction material for open wagons, in 1945 the first all-steel designs appeared. Some were truly all-steel but an interesting variation was the provision of six plank wooden doors on some versions. Batches of both fitted and unfitted vehicles were produced.

Covered goods vans

Although some measure of protection for goods conveyed in open wagons could be afforded by covering them with tarpaulins, some goods demanded better than that. The covered goods van provided protection against the weather and other hazards such as a locomotive throwing its fire when working hard. Covered vans were again used in some numbers by the pre-grouping companies but the only vans to 12 tons capacity were to come from the NER. These were built on 9 ft wheelbase wooden underframes with divided centre doors. The top portion was hung cupboard fashion and the lower were bottom hinged as on the open goods wagon. The variety of covered vans from the LNER constituents was considerable. Fitted and non-fitted versions existed, of course, and several styles of planking and door arrangements could be found. Some had no roof ventilation fitted whilst others had as many as six roof-mounted torpedo ventilators. Carrying capacity varied from 6 tons upwards. The 9 ft wheelbase underframe of timber was again common although steel underframed vehicles also existed.

The first LNER design of covered goods van featured vertical wooden planking on the sides, horizontal planking on the ends and a centre sliding door. Versions were built on wooden or steel underframes in both fitted and unfitted forms, all with a common 9 ft wheelbase. Wheels could be either spoked or three hole disc pattern and ventilation was provided via a sliding shutter on the vehicle ends. In 1934, with the decision that fitted vehicles should be built on steel underframes, a change was made to the end construction. The horizontal planking was replaced by pressed steel ends with horizontal corrugations and once again there were variations to the basic theme. Ventilation was provided by a centrally-mounted hood high up on each end. New construction continued to this design until the shortage of steel brought about during the war forced a return to horizontal wooden planking, although the steel underframe was retained. Still plagued by shortages of materials, later vans had plywood bodies and others had vertical but very narrow planking. On these matchboard vans the end planking was also vertical.

Variations on the general covered goods van design were also used for the carriage of specific traffic. These included fruit, fish and perishable traffic including meat. Bananas were conveyed in large quantities, often in complete train loads, and these vans were fitted with steam heating to assist in ripening the fruit while it was in transit. Refrigerator vans came into stock from the GNR and the LNER built further vans of 8 tons capacity up until about 1930. These were of two designs mounted on both timber and steel underframes.

Because of the perishable nature of all the goods named above they had to be conveyed quickly to their destination. To allow for fast running, either as complete trains or as additions to ordinary passenger trains, all of these vehicles were fitted with screw couplings and automatic vacuum brakes. The nightly Aberdeen–London fish trains were run at speeds better than some expresses and the sight of all those vans hurtling along behind a Class V2 must have been something to behold. It also explains some curious combinations of rolling stock as it was common to terminate a fish train of this nature with a 61 ft 6 in passenger coach of the brake composite type. This was provided not for the conveyance of passengers, but so that the guard could have a more comfortable ride, the unfortunate individual otherwise having to suffer a very uncomfortable ride in a 20 ton goods brake.

Mineral wagons

To the uninitiated the difference between an open goods wagon and a mineral wagon may be hard to distinguish. In common with other writers, I take the difference to be marked by the planking arrangements at the side doors. If the full height of the side is included in the door then it is an open goods wagon. However, if the door stops short of the top so that the top plank or planks run straight through then it is a mineral wagon. In addition many also had top-hung end doors so that they could be unloaded by tipping.

Many thousand such vehicles came into LNER ownership with carrying capacities of 8 tons and upwards. The LNER itself, along with the LMS and many private owners, adopted a design emanating from the Railway Clearing House (RCH). The need for such designs was brought about by the reluctance of many of the early railways to standardize anything with their neighbours resulting in much transhipment of goods with all the attendant inconvenience, loss and damage. The carrying capacity of these end door wagons was around 12 tons although some were as high as 18 tons, some examples of the latter coming from the NBR. Even this was increased to 20 tons when many wagons of this general type were uprated during the war. In Yorkshire and the North-east the massive coal hopper was present in large numbers and was easily distinguishable by its sloping sides. These wagons were equipped with bottom discharge doors as the NER had gone in for the installation of coaling staithes in a big way. The LNER itself added over 8,000 20 ton all-steel hoppers to the fleet, all being built by outside contractors. Although they were built to the same general specification each manufacturer incorporated detail differences, a point to be noted by the modeller.

Cattle trucks

The LNER inherited cattle trucks from all of the constituent companies. These were graded small, medium and large depending upon the inside length of the vehicle, not the size of the potential occupants! It is uncertain if the LNER actually took into stock any of the small variety but there were certainly both

An LNER-built large cattle van of 1927 together with a 20 ton 'Toad D' brake van. The latter is produced by modifying an Airfix kit of the British Rail version. Note the separate handrails on the side and the lack of handrails on the concrete platform ends.

medium and large trucks. Pre-grouping cattle trucks were mostly built on wooden underframes and, whilst some were fitted with the automatic vacuum brake, all appear to have been fitted with screw couplings. This would seem to tie in with the instruction that cattle trucks were to be marshalled next to the locomotive. Where the vehicles were fitted this increased the braking power of the train, gave the cattle a smoother ride and, even if unfitted, avoided the effect of buffering up which could be considerable at the far end of the train.

The LNER also built cattle trucks with and without automatic brakes and usually on a 9 ft wheelbase. Fitted versions also had steam heating pipes to allow them to be marshalled in passenger trains. It is interesting to note that all of these vehicles were built on wooden underframes regardless of the date of construction. Perhaps it was judged that timber stood up better than steel to the after-effects of the inevitable 'by-products' generally involved when transporting livestock. A few examples were built with a 10 ft wheelbase but by this time the traffic had reduced drastically and some of these were converted into 'flats' for the conveyance of containers.

Locomotive coal wagons

As most model railways embody a locomotive depot, or at least a shed, the operator will, no doubt, require to keep his steam locomotives suitably fuelled. The LNER, and its constituents before it, hauled its own coal from the pithead and specially allocated wagons were used for this, usually labelled LOCO or in some cases LOCO COAL, in large letters. Some of these wagons were old mineral wagons that had ended their revenue earning days and many lasted on this duty long after they would otherwise have been withdrawn. Other wagons had been built specifically for this task, including some large 20 ton versions in both timber and steel. The LNER went on to build its own wooden wagons to 20 tons capacity on steel underframes. Later still it acquired some all-steel versions from outside contractors. All types had two sets of doors on each side and the initial design had an end door as well.

As well as moving huge quantities of coal for industrial and domestic use, the LNER also moved coal for its own purposes. On the left an LNER purpose-built 20 ton Loco Coal wagon and on the right an ex-NBR 16 ton wagon now being used for the same purpose.

Goods brake vans

Prior to grouping, and unlike the ordinary wagon or van which found its way all over the system, the brake van tended to stay on its own territory. After 1923 the movements of these vehicles became more widespread. Various versions existed, including four, six and eight-wheeled vehicles and all had the same general design of body. A central body was flanked at either end by a verandah on most designs but some had a verandah at one end only. Photographic evidence would suggest that the majority of these vans were unfitted which would tally with the relatively small number of automatic vacuum brake wagons and vans that came into LNER ownership.

The first design of LNER brake van contained many of the features to be found in the NER 10 ton four-wheeled van. Known as the 'Toad B', this van had vertical wooden planking, was carried on a 10 ft 6 in wheelbase steel underframe and had a large timber ducket each side. Some were fitted with sanding gear but were not fitted with automatic vacuum brakes. A development of the 'Toad B' was the 'Toad E' which followed the same general outline but had much smaller duckets manufactured out of pressed steel. The problems that could be encountered by the guard, particularly at the end of a long loose-coupled goods train, have already been mentioned. To try to overcome these problems the LNER introduced a long-wheelbased van in 1929 known as a 'Toad D'. The body outline was similar to the 'Toad E' but the longer underframe had end platforms of steel plate and a wheelbase of 16 ft. All vans built for LNER use were fitted with automatic vacuum brakes but some vans supplied to the Cheshire Lines Committee had hand brake only. In LNER ownership all brake vans, fitted or unfitted, were painted red oxide and the occasional models of grey unfitted vans that appear from time to time from the ready to run manufacturers are not based upon prototype practice. As usual the term 'standard' only applies to general outline and the 'Toad D's were no exception. Various external differences should be noted by the modeller. End doors could be all timber or half glazed, end lamp brackets were to be found in various combinations and positions, whilst the steel end platform plate was replaced by a concrete slab during the war due to the shortage of steel. The 'Toad D' was adopted as a standard design by British Railways but some detailed changes were made. By identifying these the origin of any van can easily be established. On the BR version the end platforms were equipped with handrails, the footsteps were longer, extending to below the headstocks and the arrangement of roof ventilators and stove chimney seems to have become diagonally reversed.

Model wagons, vans and brake vans

For many years the LNER modeller had to put up with almost any wagon lettered NE, the prototype accuracy being doubtful to say the least. In recent years, however, the situation has improved and quite a good selection of ready to run models to 4 mm scale are available. These include:

Mainline

One plank & container	20 ton hopper	16 ft brake van
Three plank open	Seven plank loco coal	

Three vehicles from the Mainline stable. The container and lowfit are beautifully executed as is the three plank open. Note the late and early styles of lettering on these vehicles. The 20 ton 'Toad' brake van is another matter and actually represents the British Rail development of the LNER design.

Dapol (Airfix)

Seven plank open	Five plank open (grey)	Five plank open (oxide)
Lowmac		

Wrenn

21 ton hopper

Hornby

'Toad D' brake van	Refrigerator van

Farish

Five plank (oxide)

In addition to the above there is an ever increasing number of kits so that there is really no excuse for not running proper goods trains. The one vehicle not well represented is the 'Toad D' brake van. Usually this is simply the BR version thinly disguised in LNER livery. Fortunately the old Airfix kit, although out of production, is still available over the counter and may well be re-introduced into the Dapol range. This kit makes no pretence to represent anything other than the BR version but it is a simple matter to convert it into the earlier 'Toad D' as follows.

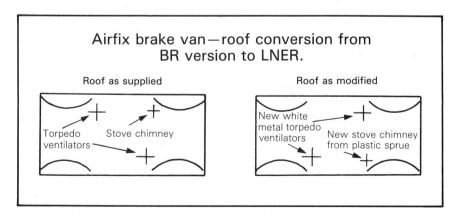

Airfix brake van—roof conversion from BR version to LNER.

Roof as supplied

Torpedo ventilators
Stove chimney

Roof as modified

New white metal torpedo ventilators
New stove chimney from plastic sprue

Variations on a theme — pair of 'Toad D' brake vans showing detailed differences in lamp brackets and doors.

The moulded torpedo ventilators should be filed off together with the stove chimney. These should be refitted as per the drawing. File off the handrails on the 'concrete' slab ends. Shorten the footsteps by 5 mm each end and divide the horizontal handrail into three sections. Also remove the small hand grabs by the ducket and reposition closer in. With reference to photographs decide upon what kind of door to fit and also the position and number of lamp brackets. Cut the moulded lamp brackets away from the end pillars.

The earlier versions where the steel plates were fitted instead of the concrete slabs are also easily represented. Mark off the body end position on the floor moulding and saw the outer end off this moulding. The vehicle is completed according to the instructions and a piece of plastic card sheet cemented over the gap left by the shortened floor moulding.

An even easier conversion concerns the old Triang 50 ton bogie brick wagon. Apart from the fitting of vacuum brake pipes and changing the wheels, all else is achieved in the paint shop. All of the necessary lettering is available on the PC LNER goods vehicle sheet of Pressfix transfers so that the hardest part is done for you. A comparison photograph of two of these vehicles, before and after, is illustrated.

A paint shop conversion. The original bright red Triang model of the 50 ton brick wagon in the foreground is actually very accurate. Repainted in LNER livery, the wheels changed and vacuum brake pipes fitted, the wagon is transformed.

Shorn of the various loads with which it is supplied, the Airfix BR 'Lowmac' machinery wagon is very like the LNER MAC NV, the sort of vehicle that might well have been seen on minor lines to convey farm implements.

Finally, don't forget that vehicles from other railways should also be represented. Those of the LMS would predominate as that railway shared a common border with the LNER. However, studies of photographs of goods trains will show that wagons from the SR and GWR also found themselves on LNER metals and travelled many miles from their parent system. The predominance of vehicle types on other railways was similar to that on the LNER so that open wagons and covered vans would again be common. All of the constituent companies of the LNER, with the exception of the NER, had registered with them goods vehicles belonging to private owners. These too should be represented and would come in the main from the local area. Some private owners only possessed a few vehicles but they did tend to go in for quite colourful liveries, all of which can add a welcome splash of colour to an otherwise drab train.

Remember also that the loose-coupled goods train was a clumsy animal to handle from the driver's point of view and was not marshalled in quite such a

A 1938-built fitted open wagon. It is fitted with an automatic vacuum brake and painted in bauxite. Don't forget the private owner wagon, this one is from a Peco kit and helps to lend colour and variety.

muddled fashion as might at first appear. Whenever possible fitted stock was marshalled next to the locomotive, to provide the best possible braking power. Hazardous goods were also marshalled acccording to strict rules which is why a train of petrol tankers, for example, will aways have at least one 'barrier wagon' or van between the main train and the locomotive. The purpose of this of course is to act as a shock absorber in the event of the whole train coming to a violent stop such as in a collision.

The study of goods vehicles and goods trains is a fascinating subject in its own right and a well made and properly constituted train can be a joy to behold and every bit as attractive as the more glamorous passenger train.

Chapter 6

Buildings and lineside

When the LNER was formed in 1923 it took under its wing the structures and practices carried out by its constituents. These railways themselves were of course also made up of other once individual railways. The result was that few if any of the LNER structures, with some exceptions amongst signal boxes, permanent way huts etc, could be said to conform to a standard design. Buildings, and in particular stations, often had to be tailored to fit a particular site and as many of these were built by contractors they too imposed their individual style. Very few new stations were built by the LNER although the opportunity to modernize some was taken usually in conjunction with other engineering work such as the improvement of a track layout. The various constituent companies themselves did however exhibit certain characteristics which can be considered to be broadly typical. Building materials tended to be those readily available to the line of the railway.

A typical LNER trespass notice bolted to a length of old rail.

Left A nice platform detail, the NBR quatrefoil contains the partially obscured company lettering whilst the lettering around the top enjoins the user to 'keep the pavement dry'.

Right The kind of station view from which a modeller can glean much information. Note seats, columns, footbridge, ticket gate, clock, bookstall, gas lamps and structural details. All now demolished and gone forever.

Station buildings

Great Northern Railway
Buildings were constructed of brick, stone or timber. South of Peterborough yellow brick predominated whilst stone was a common material in the West Riding of Yorkshire.

North Eastern Railway
Buildings were constructed of brick or stone with a high number of individual styles. Of all the constituent companies the NER had the largest number of overall platform canopies.

North British Railway
With one exception the NBR style of building was widely diverse, materials being of brick, stone and timber. The exception was the West Highland Line where timber was used in the style generally understood as 'Swiss chalet'.

Great North of Scotland Railway
Again diverse in style, buildings were of timber construction in the main although stone was also used.

Great Eastern Railway
The styles of building were generally fewer than elsewhere on the LNER. Brick was widely used with a small number being of timber construction.

Great Central Railway
Building styles were split geographically, those of the London Extension using brick with buildings being to a standard design. The trans-Pennine line of the former MS&LR however went in for a variety of styles, brick, stone and timber all being used. Timber proved to be a particularly useful material where the line ran through areas prone to the effects of mining subsidence. A few examples of overall platforms roofs existed.

Station layouts
Great Northern Railway
The predominant style was for platforms to flank the main running lines with, at larger stations, bay platforms in both up and down directions.
North Eastern Railway
Similar in layout to the GNR.
North British Railway
Many of these were of the island design with terminal bays at the larger stations. The island platform was particularly favoured on the West Highland Line.
Great North of Scotland Railway
At major stations platforms flanked running lines but this railway also possessed many miles of single track line. Some intermediate stations were provided with passing loops and the loops themselves were sometimes provided with platforms.
Great Eastern Railway
Similar to the GNR and NER.
Great Central Railway
Similar to the GNR and NER on the lines of the former MS&LR but island platforms were favoured on the London Extension.

Signal boxes and signals
Great Northern Railway
Signal boxes were variously constructed of brick, timber or stone with steep pitched roofs and gable ends. They also had horizontal sliding windows, ornate barge boards and were fitted with finials.

Signal posts were of timber, concrete or iron lattice construction. Concrete posts

Left *Platform detail — the internal footbridge is reached by a ramp rather than the more usual steps. The canopy construction is of interest, as is the ornate column.*

Below Right *A typical NBR signal box, brick built and with a hipped roof, at Alloa East Junction.*

Below *A three doll lattice bracket signal at Fort William. The original lower quadrant arms have been replaced by upper quadrants but the ball and spike finials have been retained.*

were flat capped but other styles had a ball and spike finial. The centre pivoted type of somersault signal arm was a GNR feature.

North Eastern Railway

Signal boxes were of many different patterns and changed in construction along the length of the line. Gable ended brick and timber boxes were common at the southern end of the line giving way to stone boxes with hipped roofs at the northern end.

Signal posts were often of iron lattice construction but timber was also used. Finials were ball and spike, the latter being taller than elsewhere. The slotted post signal was a feature of the NER.

North British Railway

Signal boxes were of brick or timber with flattish pitched roofs devoid of finials. Individual sliding sash windows which moved vertically were also fitted.

Signal posts were of iron lattice construction with a finial of cruciform ball and spike. In addition, the NBR shape of spectacle plate was of a distinctive pattern. From an engineering standpoint it seemed as if there was almost no limit to the height of lattice post signals, some extremely high ones being found on the NBR. Where high posts were installed it was customary to carry out lamp servicing by winding the lamp up and down by means of a winch and ladders were not fitted.

Great North of Scotland Railway

Signal boxes were of various designs including all timber, all brick, or timber on a stone base, the latter style dating back to early days. Roofs were quite steep with hipped or gabled ends. Signals were similar to the iron lattice pattern used by the NBR with lower quadrant arms and ball and spike finials.

Great Eastern Railway

Signal boxes were commonly of all timber construction but there were also a number with brick bases. Roofs were usually low pitched with plain barge boards. Finials were not fitted and boxes had horizontal sliding windows.

Signals were constructed with wooden posts but some were made of concrete under LNER ownership. Some signal posts were flat capped and others had ball and spike finials.

Great Central Railway

Signal boxes on the London Extension were similar to the design of box used on the GNR, roofs however had a flatter pitch. On other parts of the system boxes had hipped roofs. Signals had mostly wooden posts with a scattering of iron lattice or concrete examples.

London & North Eastern Railway

The inherited signal pattern continued in use and where it was necessary to replace worn arms this was usually done with the upper quadrant style, mounted on the original post or doll. Where the entire signal had to be replaced a plain tubular post with a flat cap was used. Some notable and fine examples of signal gantries were to be found on the LNER, those at York and Newcastle often being seen in photographs.

Footbridges

Lattice footbridges, both straight and curved, could be found all over the LNER.

One of the few visible signs of what was once the Corstorphine Branch. A fine example of a lattice footbridge.

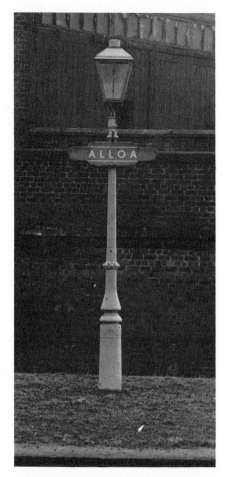 

Details for the modeller. Two lamp posts of identical design, but fitted with different lamps.

They could be made out of iron, steel or timber. Some of the timber ones were painted whilst others were left in their natural state and coated with preservative oil. The curved version was common on the GNR, GCR, NER, NBR, and on LNER-built examples. Examples built of steel could be found on the GNoSR and NER, some of the latter having a canopy over.

Turntables

Turntables are one of the more difficult features to represent in model form as there is no doubt that they do take up a lot of room. This limitation also applied in real life and some loco depots had turntables unsuitable for the locos that were eventually shedded there although they were no doubt adequate when they were installed. The fitting of new turntables was not always possible, especially where they were already occupying a cramped site. In these cases it was the practice to turn locos on a convenient triangular track layout or for them to be run light to a larger turntable where this was close to hand. Yet again it is hard to find a common or standard diameter of turntable, some odd sizes obviously being the biggest that would fit into the space available. A few examples are given below:

Gorton Loco Depot	65 ft
Sheffield Victoria	55 ft 2 in
Leicester Central	70 ft
Retford	55 ft
Wigan	50 ft
Southport	60 ft
Macclesfield	44 ft 10 in
Perth	52 ft
Alloa	50 ft
Haymarket	70 ft
Stirling	42 ft
Fort William	52 ft
Mallaig	51 ft

★ ★ ★

The foregoing is of necessity an abbreviated account which serves to show that the civil engineering side of the LNER was full of variety with a bewildering array of

A timber lamp hut. The way the chimney stack is incorporated is interesting, as is the ornate style of chimney pot also evident on the signal box.

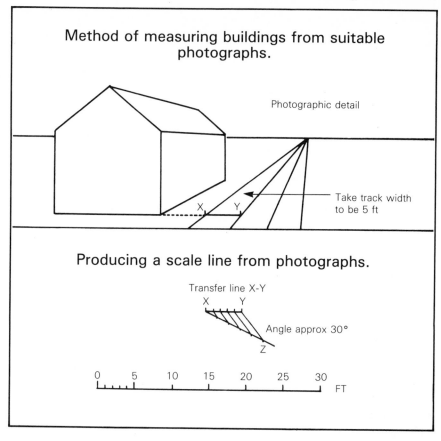

Method of measuring buildings from suitable photographs.

Photographic detail

Take track width to be 5 ft

Producing a scale line from photographs.

Transfer line X-Y

Angle approx 30°

0 5 10 15 20 25 30 FT

Use the calibrated line X-Y to produce a scale. Mark off line X-Z in convenient equal divisions. Join points Y and Z and all points on X-Z to top line so that all lines are parallel. Each division on line X-Y now equals 1 ft and the whole line 5 ft. The wall height, height to roof peak and width can now all be measured.

styles. To model a particular building or station it is essential to consult a number of good photographs, preferably dated and showing more than one elevation. Unfortunately building drawings seem to be few and even fewer are drawn to a convenient railway scale. However, all is not lost as there is a way of producing acceptable models based upon photographs.

Before modelling begins it is necessary to convert the photographic detail to a drawing which need not be terribly detailed but serves to reveal the main dimensions. Nearly all railway photographs contain visual clues to enable a rough judgement to be exercised so that it is easy to see that a building is small, medium or large. The modeller however has to do better than that and what is needed is a view which clearly shows a piece of track viewed along its length.

Now you have a fixed dimension anywhere along the track, namely 4 ft 8½ in or, for this purpose, work to 5 ft over the outer edges of the rails. To illustrate the method in practice consider a view of a simple gable ended single road loco shed photographed from track level with the track passing close to it and parallel to its length. With a pair of dividers measure off the distance over the rails immediately opposite the closest corner of the building. This distance, no matter what size it is, represents 5 ft in full size. Transfer this to paper as a line and divide it into five using the method illustrated. Each division now represents one foot and it is a simple matter to mark off a line to represent any length you require.

Now measure the base of the shed at its closest elevation and measure this against your scaled line. Similarly measure the height of the walls and the highest point of the gable end. Measure and mark off the position and size of any doors, windows etc. You now have the basic dimensions of both ends of the building. The length of the shed can now be found by selecting a good side view and it does not matter if the object is of a different size to other views. The one dimension now known, whatever the size of the photograph, is the height of the walls. Say, for example, it is 15 ft. Again measure this with your dividers, transfer that distance onto paper, divide into fifteen and extend to the length required. You now have a measure against which to gauge the length of the shed together with the size and location of doors, windows, ventilators or whatever. It is now a simple task to convert the measurements you have in feet and inches into your chosen railway scale. All that remains then is to build it.

It would be wrong to pretend that this method is going to produce an absolutely true scale model but if you work carefully it will be as near as makes no difference. The finished article may well be a few inches out but then again if you could measure the original building you would more than likely find that the builder was not accurate to a fraction of an inch either, assuming he had any drawings in the first place. Even allowing for errors, if you have measured carefully the error should be constant so that your building will, none the less, be in proportion. The model of Alloa loco shed illustrated in this book was constructed purely from photographs long after the shed itself had disappeared. The drawing of the former GCR footbridge also shown was similarly produced. In this case the first dimension to be established was that between the brick pier and the platform edge which was scaled to ten feet. From that one dimension all else was drawn. Some weeks after it was completed a colleague was able to visit the area and carry out some measurements on the actual site. The distance was exactly ten feet.

Even if suitable photographs cannot be found for all elevations a good guide to dimensions can be gained from other clues. A locomotive poking out of a shed will give a good guide as to door size for example, the height of the loco above rail level being not too difficult to establish from other sources. Having mastered the technique it can be used to measure all sorts of structures from tunnel mouths to signal posts. If it is intended to model a large or complex building then it would be advisable to construct a rough card model. Doors and windows need only be

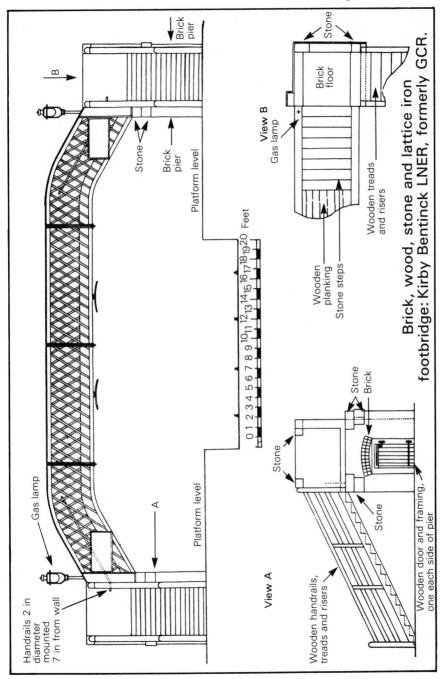

Handrails 2 in diameter mounted 7 in from wall

Gas lamp

Platform level

Platform level

A

B

Stone

Brick pier

Brick pier

Stone

View B

Gas lamp

Brick floor

Stone

Wooden treads and risers

Wooden planking

Stone steps

View A

Wooden handrails, treads and risers

Stone

Stone

Stone

Brick

Wooden door and framing, one each side of pier

0 1 2 3 4 5 6 7 8 9 10 11 12 13 14 15 16 17 18 19 20 Feet

Brick, wood, stone and lattice iron footbridge: Kirby Bentinck LNER, formerly GCR.

Constructed in plastic card with individually fitted roof tiles, this model of Alloa loco shed was constructed from measurements taken from photographs and converted to scale as described.

pencilled in. Position the model on the layout, if it looks right, then it is right and building can commence.

LNER painting schedule

Assuming that the model has been successfully constructed it will be necessary to paint it to represent the original and to blend in with the model layout. The LNER set out a full and comprehensive schedule for painting buildings and structures. This includes many references to the undercoat to be used and the number of coats to be applied. The modeller, however, is not likely to want to follow this pattern to the letter so what is given here is an abbreviated version.

Station buildings, canopies, columns etc

Large roofs, roofs over platforms, awnings and verandahs, all above capitals of columns, including iron work inside and out — deep cream.

Low columns, 8 ft or less to capital — dark brown.

High columns, base to about 4 ft 6 in high — dark brown with 1½ in black band then middle buff to top of capital.

Cornices, facias, barge boards and mouldings, vertical boarding in screens etc — deep cream.

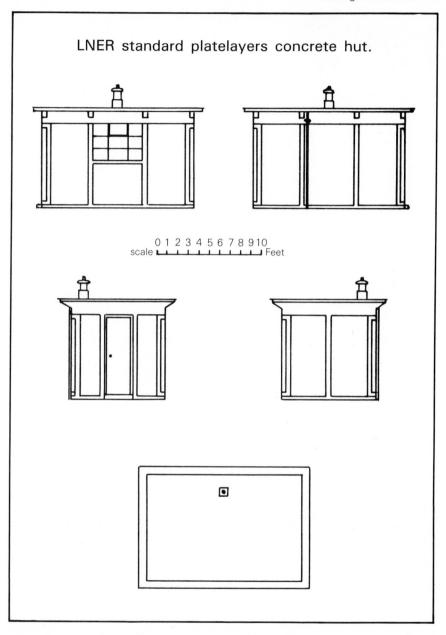

LNER standard platelayers concrete hut.

0 1 2 3 4 5 6 7 8 9 10
scale |⎯⎯⎯⎯⎯⎯⎯⎯⎯⎯| Feet

This design of hut replaced many of the older wooden types which abounded. Of modular construction, it could be erected as a single or double length unit.

Outside of doors and window and door frames — dark brown.

Window sashes — deep cream.

Platform seats, clock frames — dark brown (although the latter could also be black).

Timber station buildings

Bulk of woodwork — deep cream.

Dado and plinth, to about 4 ft high — dark brown with $1\frac{1}{2}$ in black line then deep cream above.

Gutters, spouts, gas and water pipes — chocolate oxide or deep cream depending upon the background colour.

Lamp posts, lamp brackets and brackets to notice boards — dark brown.

Lamps — outside dark brown, inside white.

Urinals (wholly cast iron) — dado dark brown with $1\frac{1}{2}$ black line, upper part rock granite and varnished, ceiling lime-washed.

Urinals (open) — stalls and troughs tar paint, walls lime-washed.

Note Where walls of urinals and closets were painted a fine sand was blown onto the surface whilst the paint was still wet to help discourage graffiti.

Internal painting

Window sashes and fanlights — deep cream.

Woodwork of doors and window frames — dark brown.

Walls and screens — dado to about 4 ft high dark brown with $1\frac{1}{2}$ in black line then deep cream above.

Ceilings, cornices and friezes — broken or off white.

Fixed seats in waiting rooms — dark brown.

Name and notice boards

Station name boards — ground black with white inner border and black outer border, lettering white.

Supporting posts of name or other boards — from ground or platform level to about 2 ft 6 in high, black, remainder white.

Refreshment room, hotel, trespass and other notices — white lettering on a black background.

Fire and emergency notices — white lettering on a red background.

Timetable and bill boards — heading white lettering on a red background, remainder, including border, black.

Milepost and gradient boards — black lettering on white background.

Motor notices on bridges — white lettering and border on a red background.

Commercial and entertainment boards — heading white lettering on light brunswick green background, border black.

Goods warehouses, sheds, stables, workshops etc

Skylights, windows and doors — as for station buildings.

Exterior of timber walls — as for station buildings.

Roofs and walls inside — lime-washed.

Iron work on roofs — deep cream.

Columns, gutters, spouts and down pipes — as for station buildings.

All other iron work — black.
All other woodwork — deep cream.

Corrugated iron buildings
Walls inside and out, roofs inside — deep cream.
Roofs outside — tar paint.

Offices
As for station buildings.

Signal boxes
Outside — as for station buildings.
Windows and doors — as for station buildings.
Stairs — dark brown.
Gutters, spouts and down pipes — as for station buildings.
All other iron work — black.
Name boards — as for station buildings.
Inside — dark brown to sill level then $1\frac{1}{2}$ in black line, deep cream above and
ceilings white.

Platelayers' huts and fog cabins
Tarred outside (timber or corrugated iron), lime-washed inside.

Loco water columns and stand pipes
Dark brown.

Fire appliances
Mains and hydrants — red.
Boxes and buckets — white inside, red outside, top beading, bottom rim and
handle black and all lettering black.

Bridges, turntables, fences and gates etc
Girders, handrails etc — chocolate oxide and graphite.
Iron and steel footbridges — chocolate oxide and graphite.
Timber footbridges — deep cream or unpainted and treated with preservation oil.
Water tanks — dark brown.
Engine turntables — dark brown or tar paint.
Station fences — deep cream with black iron work.
Ticket barrier (under cover) — dark brown.
Iron railings — dark brown or tar paint.
Level crossing gates — white with a red target and black ironwork.
Buffer stops — at platform ends beam face red, others beam face white.
Loading gauges — from ground level to 2 ft 6 in black, remainder white with black
iron work.

This colour scheme was used until about 1937 or slightly later. Sources differ as to
when the first major change took place, some say 1937 and others 1939. At around
this time the dark brown was replaced by green and the deep cream retained. It is
not certain how many buildings and structures received the revised colour scheme
before all work was brought to a halt by the outbreak of the Second World War.
Examples of green and cream painting certainly existed throughout the system and
could still be seen many years after the LNER ceased to exist. For those wishing to

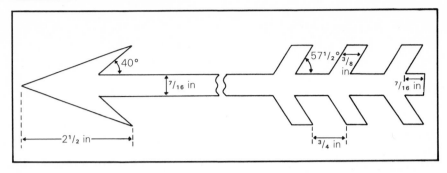

This standard arrow was the only symbol used for direction purposes on LNER premises. Where possible it was placed horizontally, but if used to point up or down a staircase it was placed at 45°. The length of the arrow was adjusted by altering the length of the shaft.

match their paint colours to the original, the British Standard Paint Numbers are as follows:

BS 12b dark brown

BS 25b light brunswick green

BS 53b deep cream

It should be remembered of course that atmospheric conditions would markedly alter the shade after prolonged exposure, particularly to direct sunlight.

There can be little doubt that all the well known and well executed model railways share a common factor — they have all been the subject of a great deal of research. Furthermore this detail has been successfully translated into miniature. A small, but well built railway is infinitely more impressive than miles of track surrounded by a few cardboard buildings. Remember that it is not advisable to attempt dead scale modelling unless it is intended to carry the principle all the way through, for example, model outside cylinder locomotives generally require a little more clearance at platform edges than the prototype does.

Chapter 7

Liveries

Pre-grouping liveries
Prior to the First World War many of the railways of Britain had used distinctive and sometimes splendidly ornate liveries for their locomotives and passenger stock. The railways which were amalgamated to form the LNER were no different and a brief summary of the liveries they used is given below.

Great Northern Railway
Locomotives: All locomotives had been grass green but during the First World War this had given way to grey for goods locomotives and a few passenger locomotives.

Passenger stock: Their livery was very similar to that finally adopted by the LNER. The GNR livery was also applied to ECJS and M&GNR stock.

Freight stock: Bodies brown red oxide with black underframes and running gear. All lettering white. Refrigerator and meat vans were white with black lettering as were gunpowder vans except that their lettering was red.

A funny locomotive in more than one sense. Class A3 Humorist *was the subject of many smoke lifting experiences in its life. Shown here with plain double chimney and large smoke deflectors, the model began life as a Hornby Class A3.*

North Eastern Railway

Locomotives: Passenger locomotives were painted in saxony green with black and white lining. Goods locomotives were black with red lining. During 1922 some of the recently acquired H&BR locomotives had been repainted in the appropriate livery.

Passenger stock: This was painted in a dark shade of crimson lake including the ends of bow ended stock. The ends of other vehicles were black whilst all roofs were white.

Freight stock: Bodies painted grey with white lettering. The underframes and running gear were black. Some brake vans were painted in red oxide.

North British Railway

Locomotives: Prior to 1914 all locomotives had been painted bronze green with red, yellow and black lining. After this date goods locomotives were painted black with double yellow lining. From 1921 two new styles were adopted, unlined green for passenger locomotives on the duplicate list and unlined black for goods locomotives.

Passenger stock: The body sides were painted crimson lake with ends black. Underframes and running gear were black and roofs white.

Freight stock: Bodywork painted grey with white lettering. Sometimes the iron work was painted black. Running gear painted black. An inverted crescent was also painted on the body together with a quatrefoil. The former contained two numbers which indicated the year of construction or last general overhaul. The quatrefoil is thought to have been an illiteracy marking.

Great North of Scotland Railway

Locomotives: These were painted in brunswick green until 1914 then black with red and yellow lining.

Passenger stock: The lower body sides were painted in a shade described as dark claret with white upper panels. Roofs were white and all else black.

Freight stock: The woodwork was painted in dark grey with the iron work picked out in black. All lettering was white. Service stock had dark red woodwork.

Great Central Railway

Locomotives: Passenger locomotives were painted in brunswick green with red, black and white lining. Goods locomotives were black with red and white lining.

Passenger stock: Lower body panels were painted chocolate brown and the upper panels in french grey although the latter was changed to cream in 1903. A further change to natural varnished wood was made in 1910. Roofs were white and underframes and running gear black.

Freight stock: These were painted lead grey with white lettering and black underframes and running gear. Refrigerator vans were a lighter grey and the white lettering was shaded black with the word REFRIGERATOR in red.

Great Eastern Railway

Locomotives: These had been painted royal blue up until the First World War when a change was made to unlined grey.

Passenger stock: Varnished natural wood was used but some new stock was painted crimson lake from 1919. Roofs were lead grey or lead oxide and underframes and running gear were black.

Freight stock: This was painted dark grey with white lettering and black underframes and running gear.

It should be noted that where dates of a change are given this does not necessarily mean that the new livery was applied universally over a short period. Much of the painting was done with great care and cleaned and looked after thereafter so that it had a long service life. Repainting usually took place during general overhauls so it could be some years before the last examples of an outdated livery actually disappeared. For example several ex-NBR bronze green locomotives came into LNER stock as did a few examples of GER blue locomotives. One brunswick green locomotive from the GNoSR survived to become LNER property while the 1914 livery could still be seen on that railway's 0-4-2T locomotives beyond 1939!

LNER liveries

Locomotives

The LNER directors wasted no time in making a decision on the new company's corporate image. The Board met at York on 31 January 1923 to view eight locomotives specially brought together for the occasion. These were:

Class C7 in NER green
Class Q6 in NER black with red lining
Class C1 in GNR green
Class O2 in black with red lining
Class C11 in NBR bronze green
Class D11 in GCR green
Class B7 in GCR black with red and white lining
Class A5 in GCR green

LNER Class A10, Sir Visto, *formerley Class A1. Rebuilt from a Hornby Class A3, the banjo dome has been replaced by an ordinary dome mounted on the second boiler ring and the eight wheeled tender converted to non-corridor version. Lettering and numbers are in Gill Sans style without shading.*

With two exceptions they were all lettered L.&N.E.R., together with large numerals on tender or tank sides. The two exceptions were that the Class O2 and C1, both painted at Doncaster, had no stops after the letters.

A further inspection was carried out at Marylebone on 22 February 1923 where the directors inspected twelve locomotives. These included Classes D11, B7, C11 and C7 already seen at York. The additional examples were:

Class B12 in GNR green
Class A5 in GNR green
Class A5 in GCR green
Class A1 in GNR green
Class B16 in NER black with red lining
Class C11 in GNR green
Class C4 in NER black with red lining
Class C7 in GNR green

The GNR livery exhibited was slightly modified as it no longer had the olive green edging. In the event this modified livery was the one chosen as the new passenger tender locomotive livery together with the former NER livery of black with red lining for tank and goods locomotives.

Meanwhile daily work went on and locomotives were emerging from the various works in their appropriate pre-grouping liveries albeit modified by the omission of previously carried coats of arms or lettering. The new style came into general use in March 1923. The lettering was $7\frac{1}{2}$ in high with large numerals and the stops omitted from L&NER. From May 1923 12 in high numerals together with the smaller letters were being used in two styles. The first was in gold for passenger locomotives and the second in yellow for goods locomotives, both beautifully shaded to the right and below. Smaller $4\frac{1}{2}$ in figures of similar style were used on buffer beams. Some tank locomotives displayed no number at the rear whilst others had it on the buffer beam or on the back of the bunker.

Between June and September 1923 the '&' was dropped and in the latter month the section suffix was adopted in $4\frac{1}{2}$ in high letters. Needless to say, with the large number of locomotives involved and the number of individual works, the new style was some time in becoming universally adopted. The former GER works at Stratford, for example, continued to paint locomotives in their grey livery with the LNER number painted in GER style and without any lettering. The final example of this did not disappear until 1932. The business of individual works failing to comply with the norm was to occur from time to time and more generally in 1946, when attempts were being made to return to pre-war standards. This made for some interesting combinations and provides the modeller with a greater variety of choice.

The green livery was intended for passenger locomotives and a general rule of thumb seems to have been used in defining these. A driving wheel diameter of more than 6 ft provided the dividing line but here again certain works included locomotives with driving wheels of considerably less. For example, Cowlairs included the Glens and others whilst the NER included classes X1, X2, and X3 as

A close-up of the front end of Humorist. *Smoke deflector plates were cut from brass sheet and fixed to cross tubes running across the smokebox. It was the only member of the class to carry this type of deflector.*

they were often used to haul the official saloon. The full list of classes painted green at this time is as follows:

A1, A2, A3

B1, B2, B3, B4, B12, B14, B17

C1, C2, C4, C5, C6, C7, C8, C10, C11

D1, D2, D3, D4, D5, D6, D7, D8, D9, D10, D11, D12, D13, D14, D15, D16, D17, D18, D19, D20, D21, D22, D23, D24, D25, D26, D28, D29, D30, D32, D33, D34, D36, D38, D40, D41, D42, D43, D44, D49

E1, E5

'901' Class

X1, X2, X3, X4

The original placing of numbers and letters was maintained until May 1928 when, with the introduction of the London–Edinburgh non-stop services, the Gresley Pacifics had their numbers put onto the cab side. The tender lettering became more centralized and increased in size to 12 in to match the numerals. This was to allow the free interchange of corridor tenders between locomotives as required. This style was then generally adopted from November 1928 although it did not begin to appear until early in 1929. In the meantime this splendid beginning had become the victim of the generally depressed economic state. In order to effect economies the number of classes to be painted green had been markedly reduced from the middle of 1928. At the same time the goods locomotive livery had been altered to unlined black although secondary passenger tender and tank locomotives still qualified for red lining. The classes which still qualified for green livery were:

A1, A2, A3

B1, B2, B3, B4, B12, B17

C1, C6, C7, C8, C11

D49

X1, X2, X3

Further classes were added to that list as they were introduced prior to 1941. They were A4, C9, K4, P2, V2 and V4. The inclusion of Class B12 in the revised list did not stop the old GNoSR works at Inverurie from turning them out in black however, although the reason for this does not seem to have been recorded. Two former GER locomotives of Class D16 also retained green livery for royal train workings and a third was similarly treated in 1933.

Locomotives fitted with cabs that were too short to accommodate full sized numerals carried versions $7\frac{1}{2}$ in or 9 in high. There were also those locomotives where an ornamental beading crossed the cab side sheets. At first experiments were conducted by placing the numbers high on the cab side above the beading or alternatively within it. Eventually a lot of these locomotives had their beading removed and the number restored to a more normal position. Locomotives with small tenders also posed a problem so the $7\frac{1}{2}$ in style of LNER was used. This was particularly prevalent in Scotland where even quite large tenders still carried this small style.

These anomalies aside, the livery style was standardized for the majority of locomotives. There were, it is true, still instances of works introducing their own variations. For example, Doncaster painted the outside cylinder covers black whilst Darlington painted them green, usually in the form of a white edged panel.

In 1935 a new livery was introduced for the Class A4 Pacifics. The first four were painted in a three-tone grey scheme with silver-grey predominant. Letters and numerals were 12 in high but were silver with blue shading. This unique livery was specially adopted to match the coaches of the 'Silver Jubilee' train. As additional A4 locomotives were built they reverted to green livery applied in two

Yet more modifications — Humorist with a GNR pattern tender with coal rails. This is basically a plastic card box which is not as detailed as a casual glance might suggest.

styles. The first carried the front end black back as far as the first boiler band thus 'squaring off' the front end and totally destroying the natural sleek look. It is believed that this was done because of uncertainty about the ability of the green paint to withstand the heat of the smokebox. This fear was apparently groundless as subsequent locomotives carried the green paint forward in the familiar parabolic curve. By the middle of 1937 another new livery had appeared, again for use on the A4s. Seven locomotives were painted in the now familiar garter blue to haul two further prestige trains, the 'Coronation' and the 'West Riding Limited'. In 1938 this livery became standard for the whole class, existing liveries being repainted as the locomotives passed through the works. The seven blue locomotives were different too, in that their numbers and letters were made from stainless steel and highly polished. They were also of Gill Sans typeface, the first occasion this had appeared on a locomotive although it had been in use for some time (since November 1932) on printed material and signs. The only other locomotive to receive garter blue livery was the former experimental 'Hush-Hush' No 10000 when it was rebuilt in A4 streamlined form to become the sole member of Class W1.

By 1941 the shortage of manpower and just about everything else was acute so from November unlined black was adopted for all classes. By July 1942 the lettering was reduced to NE on many locomotives and the formerly highly polished stainless steel embellishments were over-painted in matt yellow. The manpower shortage had some unintended effects too. Some NBR tank locomotives which had carried black livery with red lining immediately prior to 1939 were not repainted and so carried it throughout. Whether it could be seen on all of them is, of course, another question. Cleaning was given a very low priority during wartime so that even the once beautiful A4s were a sorry sight to see.

Two devices had long been familiar to the LNER traveller; the company's coat of arms and the 'totem' often found on notice boards etc. The coat of arms was only twice used on locomotives, once on Class D3 No 2000 which was kept in immaculate condition for special saloon haulage, and once on No 4472 'Flying Scotsman' when that locomotive was specially prepared for the Wembley Exhibition of 1924 and it remained on the cab side until 1928. The LNER totem in the form of a cast plate with white letters on a blue background was fitted to the bunkers of Class Q1 0-8-0T locomotives. A version painted in gilt was also used on the pioneer electric locomotive intended for use on the line between Manchester and Sheffield.

After the war was over the LNER announced that it was going to repaint all engines green except for the A4s and the solitary W1 which would again be garter blue. In the event this ambitious scheme failed to come to fruition, the various works being far too busy catching up on the arrears of repairs and maintenance. However some locomotives were repainted including nearly all of the A4s which on this occasion were all fitted with stainless steel letters and numerals. Some of the following classes were repainted green in this early bid to restore the railway to its former glory:

A1, A2, A3, A10

The LNER totem.

Top The 'medium' totem was designed for use on signs, notices, locomotives, vehicles, etc.
Above The 'light' totem was designed for use only on internally illuminated signs and external illumination with internally illuminated station entrance signs.

B1, B2, B3, B4, B12, B17
D3, D11, D16, D29
J36, J50, J69, J71, J72, J83
K2, K3, K4
L1
N2
V2, V4

The 1946 renumbering scheme, as has been stated, involved renumbering the entire stock of locomotives and in some cases appears to have out-run the supply of transfers. As a result on a number of occasions the new numbers were hand painted, often to an odd size and to a standard well below that previously employed. By December 1946 a decision had been taken to standardize on unshaded Gill Sans numbers and letters so that these too began to add variety to the styles on view.

After the war the LNER, always sensitive to the value of good publicity, made some attempt to restore the company's image to its former glory. It has always seemed odd however that one obvious opportunity was not seized. On the commendable side a decision was taken to repaint certain locomotives and then to keep them in pristine condition where they were employed on station pilot duties. Examples were included from Classes J69, J72 and J83. And yet poor old *Mallard*, surely the most prestigious A4 and the world speed record holder was left to run around in a deplorably filthy run down state, a badly hand painted 22 on her cab side and in black livery right up to the end of LNER ownership.

Before leaving the subject of locomotive liveries mention should be made of self-propelled stock. Steam railcars were initially painted teak, followed by red lower panels and cream upper panels. This was again followed by engine green lower panels and cream upper panels. A few of them were painted overall brown during the war. The few diesel railcars were painted blue and primrose in similar style, later changed to green and cream. Tyneside multiple unit electric stock was originally teak, then red and cream and finally blue and cream.

Coaching stock

Reference to the beginning of this chapter will show that, as with locomotives, the LNER inherited a good selection of coaching stock finished in a variety of liveries. An exhibition of constituents' rolling stock was held at Marylebone in February 1923 for inspection by the directors. As teak finished stock was already in use by the GNR and for ECJS stock this had to be the favourite contender. Although three of the constituent companies used crimson lake it was felt that this was too similar to that already adopted by the LMS. In addition it was known that teak body panelling did not take kindly to being painted, a fact which seems to have been forgotten in the red and cream period of British Railways.

The decision of the directors was that all general service stock would be constructed in teak and mounted on steel underframes. The external finish would be to the same high standard already evident on GNR and ECJS stock. The highly varnished and polished finish took a considerable amount of time and effort to achieve. No fewer than eighteen stages were involved and the whole process, allowing for drying time, took approximately twenty days. Coaching stock normally visited the works every three years to be rubbed down and then received a single coat of varnish. Badly stained stock was cleaned with acid to restore the colour. Although a great deal of care was taken to match the individual panels on a particular coach, strict matching was not always possible so that different tones could appear on the same vehicle and no two were exactly the same. This, together with successive varnishings, meant that the colour of the panelling became darker with the passage of time. Some of the older pre-grouping stock was eventually to become beyond remedial measures and when this happened it was painted overall in teak paint. For a while after 1923 pre-grouping stock continued to be repainted in old livery but as paint stocks ran out they were also painted with teak paint.

The mouldings and vertical casings on all corridor stock were lined out on body sides and ends. This was done with a line of primrose $\frac{3}{8}$ in wide edged on each side with a red line $\frac{1}{16}$ in wide. In practice, and bearing in mind that all of this lining was painted by hand, the actual width of these lines could vary. The lining on vertical casings terminated in a small arrow shape.

Non-corridor stock was finished using the same general techniques including, up to 1925, the body ends. Thereafter the body ends were painted plain black. Unfortunately there appears to be some doubt as to whether this type of stock was lined or not. Photographic evidence would suggest that it was, certainly in the early period. Other photographs are not quite so informative as the mouldings from natural areas of highlighting and many just give the appearance of being lined. Either way it is suggested that unless the period very close to 1923 is being modelled the lining is best left off this type of stock.

Whilst varnished teak stock made up by far the majority of coaches there were others, both of wooden and steel construction. Some of the wooden non-teak stock was painted with teak paint but later an attempt to simulate teak graining was made with varying degrees of success. The steel panelled coaches were treated in the same way but were, in the early examples at least, much more convincing. In order that they should conform visually with genuine panelled stock not only was the graining reproduced, but also the mouldings and casings. These were shaded off to represent shadow, so the study of photographs becomes interesting as it can be very difficult to identify this stock only from its appearance. There is one important point to note at this juncture. On all teak panelled stock, genuine or simulated, and on the steel panelled stock introduced post-war, the graining on the body sides below the waist was always horizontal and above the waist was vertical. On the early non-corridor stock and on all corridor stock the graining on the coach ends was all vertical. Several otherwise fine models have been made with all of the graining shown as horizontal.

The lettering and numbering of vehicles maintained the high standard set by the coachwork. Shaded letters and numerals were 4 in high and 5 in wide over the basic figure. Gold leaf transfers were used and shaded to the left and below and to the right and below. From 1923 until 1928 the 'LNER' was placed on the waist panel as near as possible to the centre of the body with the number shown twice, flanking the letters on either side. After 1928 the 'LNER' was placed as near as possible to the left hand end on the waist panel and the number on the corresponding panel on the right hand end. Doors to Guards' compartments were labelled 'Guard' in transfer letters $2\frac{3}{8}$ in by 3 in in the same style as 'LNER'. Compartment and corridor access doors were branded with the class designation, that is 1, 2, or 3 in matching style, and were transferred onto the lower door panels in numerals 7 in high excluding the shading. Note that the figure 3 was not used after 1941, the doors to third class accommodation being left blank. Special purpose vehicles such as sleeping, restaurant or buffet cars were appropriately branded in lettering the same size as that used to show class, carried on the lower body panelling as near to the centre as possible.

As with locomotive liveries the letters LNER were reduced to NE during the war. Attention to finish and lining was neglected during the war years, however the introduction of all-steel corridor stock in 1945 and later all-steel non-corridor

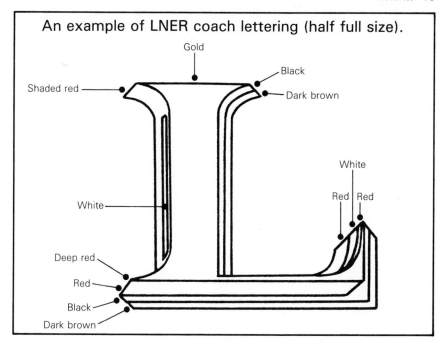

An example of LNER coach lettering (half full size).

Although LNER lettering could be clearly read at a considerable distance, the style was much more ornate than a casual glance would suggest.

stock saw a return to simulated teak finishes. This time however no attempt was made to simulate mouldings or casings but the graining was laid as for teak panelled stock.

Coach solebars, headstocks and buffer housings were painted 'teak' and varnished. The wheel centres were also finished in 'teak' paint and wheel rims were painted white. All else below the body was black. Although steam railways and white paint are not renowned for their compatability, the LNER none the less painted its coach roofs white. Needless to say this toned to light and then dark grey in service and, of course, roofs were not painted white in wartime. Toilet windows were opaque, which meant anything from white to pearl grey, as were certain windows on special purpose vehicles such as kitchen cars and the non-public portions of buffet cars.

Interior finishes

Up until the mid-1930s the interior finishes of Gresley standard stock were also teak with matt white ceilings. Compartments had the usual luggage racks and between that and the top of the seats pictures flanked an oval mirror. The interiors of the brake portion of coaches and of passenger brake vans were painted a light stone colour, again with white ceilings. By and large the interiors of the everyday stock were functional rather than fashionable. After 1930 some comparative tests were carried out using painted finishes or a rexine covering. The rexine version proved to be the more durable and was adopted generally from 1935 onwards. From the modelling aspect the provision of full interiors to coaches built to a scale of 4 mm to the foot or less is somewhat problematical. Certainly in 4 mm scale much of what is inside will not be readily visible but the fitting of seats and compartment walls is, at least, worthwhile. These can be seen and when the vehicle is viewed from a slight angle stop daylight being seen where there should not be any. On corridor stock it is also important to fit the corridor partition as large areas of this are visible. Unlike the later Thompson stock which had corridor and external windows in line, the Gresley stock more often than not only corresponded roughly, always a sore point when trying to view the railway scene through the corridor side windows.

Given that the inclusion of seating and the rest can at best only be representational the following is offered as an acceptable way of portraying them:

All-third or third section of a composite coach

Upholstery — brown/dark red/rust patterned uncut moquette, may be represented by painting with matt dark brown/red paint.

Floors — in compartments and corridors may be represented by mid brown/tan satin finish paint.

All-first and first section of composite coach

Upholstery — smoking predominantly green, may be represented by painting with matt mid-green paint. Non-smoking as above but predominantly blue.

Floors — matching carpets in compartments and corridors.

Ceilings — white enamel.

Woodwork — varnished, see section on teak finishes.

In first class compartments antimacassars approximately 12 in square were fitted to seat backs. Pictures fitted to all stock were approximately 18 in by 9 in framed.

As well as the standard livery of the general service stock the LNER also used special liveries on trains for really prestigious services or where the travelling public was being offered something a little different. An example of the latter was introduced in 1933 in the shape of tourist stock built for excursion traffic in a bid to arrest the drift away from the railway to road transport. The order was comprised of five complete trains of twelve coaches each. The external outline broke with tradition in that the roof line did not have the domed ends. The external cladding was of plywood painted in engine green below the waist and cream above with white roofs. The green and cream was carried round and across the vehicle ends. The solebars, running gear and bogies were black and wheels had their centres painted teak with white rims and axles.

The style of lettering and numbering used was the same as that used for standard stock except that it was 5 in deep, not including shading, and was elongated. Each coach in a set was individually identified by a 12 in high black letter, starting with 'A', painted in Gill Sans on a white panel to the right hand side of the outer door. The sets consisted of two open brake thirds, four twin-articulated open thirds and two buffet cars. Although intended to operate as fixed sets there are recorded sightings of isolated buffet cars being seen at Bournemouth on through trains to Weymouth.

As part of its development programme the LNER had looked at the provision of long distance, high speed train services and in particular the King's Cross to Newcastle service. Investigation of a similar German high speed service had shown that such a thing was possible except that the German service was diesel powered. After discussion it was estimated that the same could be done on the LNER by using Gresley Pacifics and a purpose built train. So it was that in 1935 there burst upon an unsuspecting railway world the 'Silver Jublilee' train together with the first of the streamliners otherwise known as Class A4. The make up of the seven coach train was two articulated twins flanking a triplet restaurant/kitchen set. These coaches were again straight roofed and the space between vehicles was covered in a rubber sheet to reduce air turbulence at speed. In addition the undergear was hidden behind iron sheeting extending down to within 10 in of the track. Of conventional construction, the framing was clad in steel panels. These were covered in silver-grey rexine and roofs were painted in aluminium. Liberal use was made of stainless steel trim around windows and door frames and for all the usual lettering and numbers. As with the tourist stock, individual coaches were identified by a 4 in high letter in blue. Normal roof destination boards were not fitted but the train carried its own identification in the form of 4 in high silver letters on a dark blue background. Underframe fairings and bogies were painted lead grey, with black wheels and axleboxes.

This startling livery was to attract a great deal of publicity which was exactly what the LNER wanted. Both the locomotive and train received special attention from the cleaners. In spite of this the rigours of running in traffic soon stained the coach livery so that within six months the set had to return to Doncaster to be sprayed silver, a process repeated at regular intervals. To meet an increasing demand an additional vehicle was built and became the centre unit of a triplet articulated set in 1938. This train ran successfully until the outbreak of war in 1939 whereupon it was stored for the duration, never to run again in its original form.

The undoubted success of this train prompted thoughts of providing additional trains of a similar nature. The construction of 27 coaches was authorized to form three trains. Two were destined for the 'Coronation' trains to be introduced in 1937 and the third train was to act as spare for all three streamlined trains.

Steel body panels on a teak frame were again employed. Like the 'Silver Jubilee' vehicles are articulated, only this time in pairs with the addition of the beaver-tail observation car. Undergear was again hidden behind a fairing. Below the waist line the bodies were finished in garter blue and above in the lighter marlborough blue. This scheme was carried around the outer ends of articulated pairs. Roofs were spray painted in aluminium, and fairings, bogies and wheels painted black. Body trim was in stainless steel, each vehicle being lettered 'CORONATION' in 6 in high Gill Sans letters on the upper portion of the panels below the waist line. This identity was also displayed across the end of the observation car. Other lettering was 4 in high. The train entered service on 5 July 1937 and consisted of two identical sets. The third set was identical in external livery but carried no train name in a permanent manner. Instead it carried its identity on standard type roof boards dependent upon the particular service for which it was deputizing. These sets were also withdrawn from use at the outbreak of war and never ran again in their original form. The two observation cars, heavily rebuilt, still exist under private ownership.

On 27 September 1937 the third of the streamlined services entered the stage. Built in identical fashion to the 'Coronation' coaches the four articulated twin sets were also externally identical except that they were lettered 'WEST RIDING LIMITED'. Also stored during the war, six of these vehicles did however emerge to be painted crimson and cream and included in the restored train of the same name when this ran again in May 1949.

The introduction of other special trains such as the 'East Anglian' and the 'Hook Continental' in 1937 and 1938 respectively carried on the intent to steadily improve services. It is interesting to speculate how far this would have gone but for the outbreak of war in 1939. In the case of these two trains however no special external livery was used although the internal appointments were better than standard stock but not quite as luxurious as in the streamlined sets. The 'East Anglian' originally consisted of six new coaches, increased to eight in October 1946. The 'Hook Continental' set consisted of ten new coaches including restaurant facilities, third and second class accommodation. The latter was designated thus to match the class system of the continental railways. In service it usually consisted of twelve vehicles being strengthened by the addition of two bogie brakes. Yet another casualty of wartime conditions, the train returned to service in November 1945.

It will be noted that no description of internal livery has been given in any great detail. There are two reasons for this. Firstly it is all well documented elsewhere (see Appendix E) and to do the subject justice would require a great many pages. Suffice it to say that it was generally designed in the spirit of the times with much use being made of aluminium, stainless steel or chrome plated fittings together with bright or heavily patterned materials for upholstery.

Freight stock

At the grouping there was a general similarity between the liveries of the constituent companies applied to freight stock. This led to the LNER standardizing its livery along similar lines which it retained for the whole of its existence, with one significant change to lettering styles. It should be noted that if the vehicle solebars were of timber they were painted the same colour as the body whereas if they were of steel channel they were painted black.

The standard livery for non-fitted wagons and vans in revenue earning service, (including loco coal and sleeper wagons but excluding brake vans) was as follows:
Bodywork, including ends — grey.
Roofs — initially white sometimes with black ventilators where fitted. Other roofs seem to have been painted grey or black when new. Later still roofs were painted the same colour as the main body.

Running gear — all black except for the handle portions of brake levers which were painted white. There is some doubt as to whether wheel rims were painted white as a matter of course or if this was done purely for photographic reasons. The standard livery for fitted wagons and vans and all brake vans was as follows:

Bodywork, including ends — brown red oxide changed to bauxite around 1940 although there appears to have been little discernable change in the actual colour.

Roofs and running gear — as for non-fitted stock.

Refrigerator vans

Body, including ends — white with ladders, stepboards and some strapping picked out in black.

Roofs and running gear — as for fitted and non-fitted stock.

Departmental stock

Body, including ends — oxford blue.

Roofs and running gear — as for fitted and non-fitted stock.

Restricted stock

A small number of vehicles were kept for use on limited trip workings or for use in yards. These were painted green but there is some evidence to suggest that some were also left in what remained of their old livery with the lettering painted on a green patch.

Breakdown cranes

Black lined out with a $\frac{1}{4}$ in red line.

Lettering

LNER ownership was indicated by the letters NE of the size 18 in by 12 in spaced equally on either side of the door. A similar style but proportionately smaller was used where space was restricted as on low-sided or flat wagons. The running number was 5 in high positioned below the E except that on vans with sliding doors the number was on the door so that it always remained visible. Below the N the wagon capacity was displayed in letters 4 in high. Where a vehicle code had been allocated, such as fish, sleeper, refrigerator, this was displayed above the capacity in letters 4 in high although on some vans, fruit for example, it was displayed on a cast plaque attached to the door. Other lettering included the tare weight in figures $3\frac{1}{2}$ in high painted onto the solebar just to the left of the right hand wheel. Smaller lettering still indicated the paint date or the last lifting date. A six-pointed star on the solebar of fitted vehicles indicated the position of the vacuum brake release cord and a W similarly positioned served the same purpose on vehicles fitted with the Westinghouse brake. All lettering was white except for that on the bodies of refrigerator vans which was black.

Minor alterations were made from time to time and about 1926 vehicles which were not for common use were lettered N, 4 in high, either on the two bottom corners of the body or alternatively on the ends of the headstocks. The wagon or van code was moved in the early 1930s to the doors of vehicles and it was at this time that the cast iron code plate was also introduced.

From 1937 new stock and that painted after that date showed a revised layout.

The company initials were reduced in size to 4 in and placed over the capacity, itself in 3 in high letters. These were placed above the running numbers which were in 4 in high numerals. The whole was placed at the lower left hand body side. At the bottom right hand corner the tare weight was displayed in 3 in high letters.

As much of the traffic carried by the LNER was coal it operated a great many open wagons. To facilitate the swift unloading of such vehicles they could be fitted with end doors, side doors, bottom discharge doors or a combination of these. To indicate the actual fit quite distinct markings were painted onto the wagon. In the case of end door wagons a white diagonal stripe was painted on the body side with the highest point at the end door position. Wagons with bottom discharge doors had a cut off V painted on the lower body side in a central position. The brake pipes of wagons and vans fitted with automatic brakes were painted black whilst those of vehicles fitted only with through pipes were painted red.

From 1943, as elsewhere on the LNER, measures were undertaken to effect economy of both materials and manpower. To this end woodwork was left in its natural state and the iron work painted black. Lettering and numbering were still painted white but were now carried on a black patch. The position of the end door was indicated by painting white the diagonal strapping at the end.

Road vehicles

No standard livery was adopted at first by the LNER for its fleet of railway goods vehicles. In general these were painted in the colour schemes used by the individual railways prior to grouping. The adoption of Gill Sans lettering in 1932 however coincided with the introduction of a standard livery. The main body colour was royal blue with white lettering. This was accompanied on suitable vehicles such as flat bed lorries by a red side stripe carrying the company name in full. Red wheel centres were also used but others appear to have been grey or black. This scheme was then adhered to throughout the remainder of the LNER's existence. In the post-war period some vehicles also carried the LNER 'totem' on front, sides and rear.

As well as the goods vehicle fleet the LNER also owned and operated a number of buses. Exact livery details do not seem to have survived but photographic evidence suggests that this was locomotive green below the waist line and white above. Where a narrow waist panel formed part of the coachwork this was finished in artificial teak graining and carried the company initials in full. This, together with the fleet running number, was applied in the same style as used on passenger rolling stock. Also owned by the LNER were a number of tramcars. These were painted in LNER teak brown with the company initials and running number in the same style as that used on passenger rolling stock.

★ ★ ★

The foregoing can be applied as a general yardstick for locomotives, coaches, freight stock and road vehicles. However it is worth remembering that with the huge numbers of stock concerned changes which occurred at specific dates could and often did take a considerable time to implement fully. Some odd results could

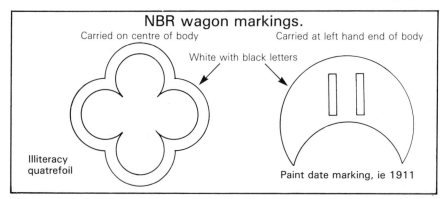

also be seen where paint had been poorly applied or applied in less than ideal conditions. It was possible to see locomotives with two numbers and wagons displaying two livery styles where the old livery showed through the new paint. Where the repainting of a locomotive class was undertaken as the opportunity arose it could be overtaken by operating expediency. For example some of the LNER Class B12s allocated to the Northern Scottish Area ended up with black livery on the locomotive and a green tender or vice versa. This was no doubt caused by a swapping of tenders in the works and the need to get the locomotive back into service.

It also appears that some vehicles became 'lost' in the system and carried outdated liveries well beyond the intended date of change. For example a Thompson post-war all-steel corridor second was photographed at Doncaster still in teak livery in 1957, some nine years after nationalization.

Before leaving the subject of liveries it should be noted that some photographs can give a totally misleading impression of the livery actually carried day by day. This mainly applies to locomotives. When new or radically rebuilt classes of locomotives were introduced it was the practice to take an official photograph for the company records. The black and white film stock of the period was not particularly good at registering tonal differences or lining, particularly red on black. In order to obtain a good register locomotives were painted in 'works' or 'photograpic' grey, very often edged in black with white lining. This was not the livery in which the locomotive entered traffic, it being washed off upon completion of the photographic task.

The majority of these photographs are easy to spot but where doubt still exists other clues must be looked for. A certain wall at Doncaster Plant for example seems to have been kept whitewashed in order to provide a suitable background. Other photographs may have had all the intrusive background detail removed altogether. Where locomotives were built by outside contractors it was often the custom to display the manufacturer's name at rail level on a suitably inscribed board or plaque. These were also to be found on offical photographs of coaching and freight stock although no special paint scheme appears to have been used in depicting their livery.

Chapter 8

Information and research

In spite of the millions of words written and the millions of photographs taken, the modeller can quite often find that whilst general information can be easily come by, detail may prove to be very elusive. For many enthusiasts, writers and photographers the existence of the railway in its comprehensive form was an unalterable fact of life. Few could have foreseen the politically inspired mayhem that was to come in the 1960s or that in a few short years much of what was of interest would be unceremoniously swept away. The sudden realization of what was really happening gave rise to the foundation of a number of specialist societies or groups. The aim of the majority of these groups was to collect and ultimately collate as much information as could be found in their chosen area of interest. Some concerned themselves with preservation projects, others with prototype information only, while yet others were comprised either wholly or in part of railway modellers. Their interest was to translate their records into model form. All of these groups are usually more than willing to share their information with others, subject to the observance of a few simple courtesies. Some of these are so obvious that it is quite incredible that they are all too often completely ignored. It is not intended to preach at this point, but experience has shown that not a lot of thought is given to the person who will deal with the enquiry. Written information in reasonable quantity will often be supplied free of charge, but this is not the same thing as being free of expense and a stamped, self-addressed envelope does not accompany enquiries as often as it should. Some individuals deal with many of these letters and the poor old 'expert' on locomotives or signalling can find himself well out of pocket at the end of it.

When making an enquiry always try to be specific. Requests for a complete list of all LNER Pacifics, with numbers and names, together with shed allocations and a list of the trains they operated are likely to receive scant attention. This was an actual enquiry received and it is hard to imagine why all this information is wanted in the first place. Perhaps the writer was just too lazy to do any work himself!

It helps too to give a brief outline of why the enquiry is being made, and to what use the information is to be put. Suppose it is needed to build a model of a particular railway location, then the recipient may well be able to assess the priorities and react accordingly. In this example a track plan would be high on the list whereas signalling details would not. It takes time to build a model railway so that it is highly unlikely that all the information would be required at once.

Remember too that the person first contacted may not himself be able to answer the query and will have to pass it on to someone who can. Having decided what information is needed, where might it be discovered? There are many avenues to be explored — you could try any or all of those suggested below and you may also be able to think of other sources related to your own area of research.

Visiting the site

This is always worth a try even if little of the railway now remains. It should still be possible to gain something of the flavour of the area and to note the local styles of architecture and building materials used. If enough of the site remains for detailed observations to be made then get onto the site itself but not, of course, without the proper authorized permission. Being a railway enthusiast, model or otherwise, does not exclude one from the law of trespass. Take a camera and a tape measure or even a home-made device which is like a surveyor's pole. This can easily be made up from timber and marked off in divisions of inches or feet. Paint each section in contrasting colours such as black/white, or anything that will show up well on film. Standing this against the object to the photographed will save hours of measuring, an important factor if the site is a large one or the weather is doing its best to ruin your efforts. Once measuring and photography is under way the activity may well attract attention and much useful information can be gleaned from talking to someone who knows the area well. The final thing to remember is that if you are lucky enough to stumble across the well preserved relic then get it on record just as soon as you can. Today's well preserved signal box is tomorrow's pile of bricks, sometimes quite literally.

Transport museums

These can be particularly fruitful areas of investigation. Often a museum will house lots of information that is not on public display, such as written records or collections of photographs. If you wish to view such a collection or search records then it is as well to write in or telephone beforehand to arrange a suitable time and obtain a name to ask for. A few days' notice has been known to produce even more information as the recipient is given time to reflect upon its nature and scope.

Beware of some things that are done however. Just because what you wish to see is in a museum does not automatically establish its authenticity! For many years the National Railway Museum at York has displayed a beautifully restored Class A4, *Mallard*. Painted in LNER garter blue and with the side valances restored, the locomotive is visually in the condition it was in when it captured the world speed record for steam traction. The record is commemorated on a pair of plaques fitted one each side of the boiler casing and it is right that in the context of a museum display that they should be there. However, the LNER never saw fit to do this and the plaques were not fitted during their ownership, but were put on by BR in March 1948. Odd examples such as this apart, the various transport museums can provide valuable information.

Preserved lines

Another useful source of information, but subject to the same cautionary remarks as above. Some of these lines take a great deal of care to preserve items in a representative state and are meticulous in their research. However it is as well to establish just what is being preserved. For example, a society may wish to repaint a locomotive in a particular livery once used by the original owners. The locomotive may however have been heavily rebuilt over the years so that the style of the locomotive and the livery may actually be many years apart. It would, of course, be totally unreasonable to expect them to 'un-rebuild' the locomotive, but you should be aware of the problem.

Public libraries

Probably the most under-used source of information. Like museums, public libraries often have a local history collection which may not be well advertised or on public display. The library can be used in two ways. If the line of research concerns something local then the local library is the one to use. If, on the other hand, it is many miles away your local library can be of assistance either by obtaining material for you or by giving you the address of the nearest library to the area of interest. A small charge may be made for copy material you may wish to retain.

Magazines and periodicals

For good commercial reasons these are wide ranging in the topics they cover but are always worth looking at. They are heavily dependent upon their contributors, who, oddly enough, have probably had just as much trouble as you in obtaining their information. These specialized magazines have a habit of turning up as back numbers at swap-meets, model railway exhibitions and even jumble sales. On these occasions it is usually possible to have a quick flick through them and this can be a good source of drawings and photographs. The current interest in railways has had one rather unfortunate side effect in that fancy prices are sometimes asked, but it is fairly easy to shop around.

The specialist groups

These have grown in scope, number and reputation over the years. Most own or have access to comprehensive records. These are usually held by individuals within the group so it may take a little time for your query to reach the appropriate person. The LNER modeller is fortunate in having a number of specialist groups to turn to. The LNER Study Group attempts to cover all areas of the line and all aspects of operation. Complementary to them are equally knowledgeable groups who confine their interest to the constituent companies. All are composed of individuals with a like-minded interest and all effort is on a voluntary basis. Their officials change from time to time and it is for this reason that no addresses are given here. They can all be contacted through the editor of your favourite model railway magazine.

Books and photograph albums

The growth in the number of railway books and albums over recent years has been phenomenal. Many early published photograph collections showed view after view of trains taken from the track side at the usual three-quarter angle and captions are often general and undated. Gradually this has changed so that many now contain shots of platform furniture, road vehicles, signals, goods sheds etc as objects of interest in their own right. Captions have become more informative and are often dated. Not perhaps the quickest way to undertake research but patience can be well rewarded. Fortunately a lot of albums are published under titles that give a good guide as to content so that it is not necessary to examine them all.

British Rail
Possessed of considerable quantities of photographs, drawings and written material, it took BR a little while to realize that these would be the subject of considerable demand by researchers and modellers alike. Limited as to resources, much remains to be done but their response to specific enquiries is usually good although it may not be instant. To alleviate the sheer volume of enquiries it is not uncommon for the specialist groups to appoint one person to act as liaison officer so that he may submit composite enquiries.

Ordnance Survey
A particularly useful source of information when it comes to track layouts. Certain areas were the subject of highly detailed maps drawn to the scale of 25 in to the mile. The date of survey is also shown. Maps may be purchased direct or obtained through a good book shop. The local library may also have copies that it is possible to examine prior to purchase.

* * *

In summary then, there are many sources of information. Remember to keep your enquiries brief and specific, enclose an SAE and at least offer to defray expenses. It is a good idea to offer what information you already possess in exchange. Most research is like trying to do a jigsaw, with maybe only a dim idea of the picture on the box lid. Missing pieces will always be gratefully received.

* * *

Researching — a practical example
It is, of course, relatively easy when writing a chapter such as this to pontificate about what needs to be done and how theoretically one should proceed, but it may be more helpful to show how it has been applied to an actual project. At the beginning of this book mention was made of a small Scottish town called Alloa which stands on the north bank of the River Forth. Long after I had ceased to live in the town I had become interested in railway modelling, so I decided to explore the history of the lines in the area with particular emphasis on the station. To begin with it was an academic project, firstly because I now lived a long way from the town and secondly there was very little available in the way of kits. The thought of having to make everything was rather daunting. As it was to turn out the intervening years were to see the introduction of a number of nice kits for NBR locomotives so the problem is at least partly solved. All it needs now is for

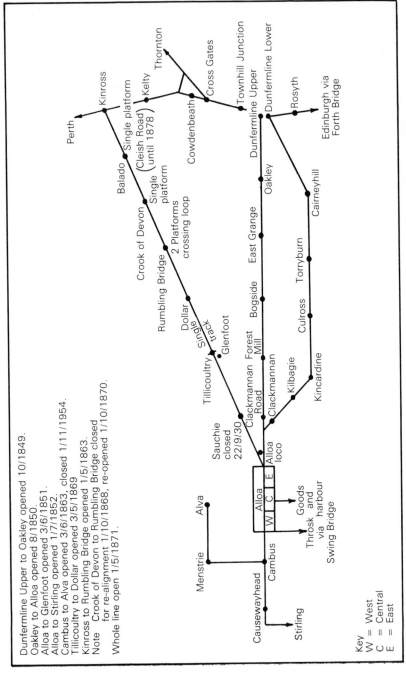

Dunfermline Upper to Oakley opened 10/1849.
Oakley to Alloa opened 8/1850.
Alloa to Glenfoot opened 3/6/1851.
Alloa to Stirling opened 1/7/1852.
Cambus to Alva opened 3/6/1863, closed 1/11/1954.
Tillicoultry to Dollar opened 3/5/1869
Kinross to Rumbling Bridge opened 1/5/1863.
Note Crook of Devon to Rumbling Bridge closed
       for re-alignment 1/10/1868, re-opened 1/10/1870.
Whole line open 1/5/1871.

Key
W = West
C = Central
E = East

No location should be modelled in isolation. A simple diagram like the one shown here will help you to understand where the trains and traffic came from and went to and why.

some enterprising manufacturer to produce a few NBR coach kits!

By way of example and illustration Alloa is as good as any as it shows what can be done where the location is neither well known nor documented. As a prototype for a model railway it offers one seldom found advantage — the main station area is bounded to the north and south by retaining walls, to the east and west by road overbridges. This is often the arrangement adopted by modellers, particularly when building a freelance layout, to define the extremities of the model. Unfortunately when translated into model form it does come out rather large, even in 4 mm scale, but could suit a model railway club as a project.

The first move was to purchase a 25 in to the mile Ordnance Survey map. These are highly detailed and as luck would have it the date of survey on my copy was 1948, right at the end of the LNER period. The map showed the location of all turnouts and crossovers which was just as well as I had last seen the actual location many years before. Some time later a planned visit to Edinburgh threw up the chance to spend a day at Alloa. A letter was written to British Railways, Scottish Region requesting a track permit and outlining what it was I wanted to do and for what purpose. The permit was duly received in the post a few days later. Prior to the visit a lot of time was spent looking at the map to establish exactly what needed to be recorded, assuming it was still there. This planning is important as it reduces wasted time and ensures that nothing vital is missed. A point to bear in mind when the chosen subject is unlikely to be visited again for some time.

The appointed day duly arrived and in the company of my father-in-law, the late J. G. Gore, the photographer in the family, I presented myself at the booking office. Passenger services in the hands of DMUs were in their last dying months and some track had already been lifted but the original layout remained visible. After introducing ourselves to the station master and explaining what it was we intended to do, we received a safety briefing from him and were then let loose upon the property of BR. As well as a camera, a couple of lenses and several rolls of film we were also armed with a tape measure, pens, pencils and a large notebook. Unless you are prepared to spend hours photographing every little detail then some sketching is necessary otherwise there will be no record of such details as stone carving or the style of window mouldings. The day was well spent photographing, sketching and measuring, and enough data was obtained to enable other detail to be deduced at a later stage. When the films were processed it was obvious that this part of the operation had been satisfactory but lots of effort still needed to be expended to convert what I had into a form suitable for use in modelling.

Using the aforementioned Ordnance Survey map, a diagram to a larger scale was prepared of the central station area and the various noted details transferred to it. This is illustrated here and together with the photographs obtained provides quite a comprehensive record, sufficient anyway on which to base a model railway. Research was now broadened to ascertain the place of the railway in its location, where the traffic came from and what industries were served. In fact several lines of enquiry were going on at once. The first of these involved writing to several railway photographers who were known to have worked in the area asking

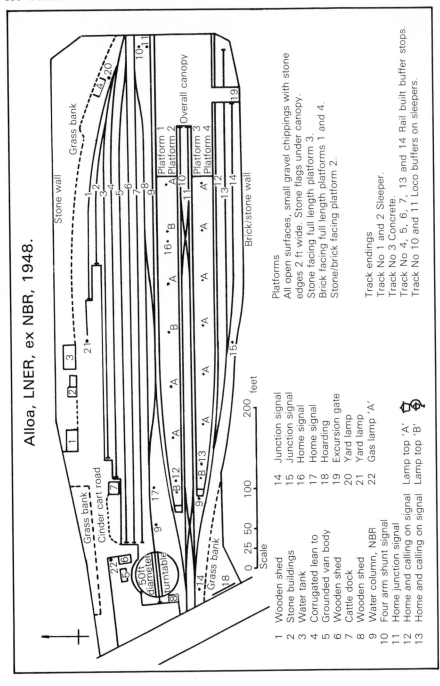

Alloa, LNER, ex NBR, 1948.

Platforms
All open surfaces, small gravel chippings with stone edges 2 ft wide. Stone flags under canopy.
Stone facing full length platform 3.
Brick facing full length platforms 1 and 4.
Stone/brick facing platform 2.

Track endings
Track No 1 and 2 Sleeper.
Track No 3 Concrete.
Track No 4, 5, 6, 7, 13 and 14 Rail built buffer stops.
Track No 10 and 11 Loco buffers on sleepers.

Scale
0 25 50   100   200 feet

1   Wooden shed
2   Stone buildings
3   Water tank
4   Corrugated lean to
5   Grounded van body
6   Wooden shed
7   Cattle dock
8   Wooden shed
9   Water column, NBR
10 Four arm shunt signal
11 Home junction signal
12 Home and calling on signal
13 Home and calling on signal

14 Junction signal
15 Junction signal
16 Home signal
17 Home signal
18 Hoarding
19 Excursion gate
20 Yard lamp
21 Yard lamp
22 Gas lamp 'A'

Lamp top 'A'
Lamp top 'B'

specifically for station area pictures and in particular any showing trains or stock. All replied and several were able to help. It is also a matter of record that where a charge was made it was very reasonable. At the same time a plea for assistance was placed in the 'Enquiry Corner' of the magazine *Railway Modeller* and that too was to produce a small but worthwhile response. Gradually a picture was beginning to emerge and locomotive types and stock were identified.

As well as these avenues of exploration a careful eye was kept open for back numbers of such magazines as *Trains Illustrated* and this too produced a number of equally good photographs and a couple of pertinent articles.

Having allowed time to digest what information had been gathered to date thoughts turned to other as yet untried sources. My local library provided the name and address of the Clackmannanshire District Librarian and a letter of enquiry was directed there. This was to be one of those occasions where a simple letter was to provide information well beyond that which might have been expected. A gentleman by the name of Adrian Ure had worked in the library at Alloa as part of his studies while at St Andrews University. The result of his labours was a publication held by the library and entitled *Local Railways, The Early Days 1850–1885*. So, there it was, a well researched and highly informative account of the railway from day one. I have never met Mr Ure but, Sir, you have my eternal gratitude. The library was, in addition, able to supply copies of a couple of early photographs. Other interesting items were by now coming to light such as the recorded sightings of Pacifics on diverted trains due to a derailment at Inverkeithing on the east coast main line on 6 March 1959.

Some time later it proved possible to pay a half day visit to Alloa station and the opportunity was taken to collect more information and to confirm other details. By this time the station had lost its passenger services, a lot more track and the buildings were boarded up. It was during this visit that an amusing incident occurred. Whilst standing on one of the overbridges doing some sketching I was accosted by a rather irate lady and treated to a diatribe on the state of the area in general, the state of the station in particular and the vast quantities of weeds present. Reasonably well dressed and armed with a clip board I suppose I must have looked fairly 'official' to her and she took the opportunity to berate me roundly for everything from the weather to the price of fish, or so it seemed at the time. A quick decision was reached to make all the right noises including a promise to see if I could do something about it. This is one of those occasions when the truth is better left unsaid. After all, how do you explain that you are really some sort of nut trying to turn back the clock and that the present state of affairs, whilst regrettable, is totally beyond your control?

That these two visits were made when they were turned out to be fortuitous as a fleeting visit paid recently showed all but the main station block demolished. The station in all its glory, as a model, remains to be built, perhaps a project to be undertaken in retirement. Astute readers will, no doubt, have noticed that amongst the locomotive illustrations there is a distinct Scottish bias although I have tried to keep this to a minimum. The Sentinel-Cammell steam railcar, *Fair Maid*, is just such an example but it is also representative of the others of its class used elsewhere on the LNER. It is also included as a piece of pure nostalgia as I have rather dim memories of having ridden on it on more than one occasion.

As I said at the beginning it is all very well to pontificate about how things should be done, but I hope that the latter part of this chapter illustrates that it does work in practice. Obviously the technique will vary depending on exactly what is being researched but the principle holds good in every case.

Chapter 9

Modelling techniques

Unlike some hobbies it is possible to practise the art of railway modelling and still remain part of the family on a social basis. Because much of what is to be done is relatively small and easily handled it is simple to make a handy sized portable work surface which can be used with equal facility in the arm chair or alongside the layout. Remember that no extensive workshop facilities are really necessary to produce first class models. True, there are those fortunate enough to possess precision lathes etc, but remember too that they probably did not start off with such exotic equipment. So, what is required to make a start?

First of all a good, flat and square work surface is essential. Do not fall into the trap of using a piece of hardboard, plywood, or any other material, the surface of which will eventually become badly scored with continuous use. Sooner or later your knife blade will fall into and then follow one of the previously made cuts and ruin your work. It is well worth investing in a piece of good quality plate glass, say 12 in by 12 in, and backing this with a suitable material such as hardboard. Between the backing and the glass insert a piece of thick paper or thin card, previously marked out with some useful guide lines. Seal it around the edge with tape and there you have your instant and highly portable work surface. Note that

A simply made portable work surface. The patterns under the glass are to assist in lining up during model building and can, of course, be drawn to any style. The black area is used when marking out transparent material, clear plastic for example.

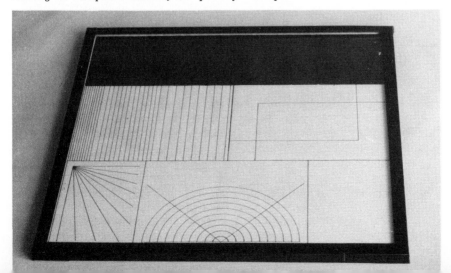

on the example illustrated an area has been coloured black, a useful addition when working on transparent materials where it is required to see scribed lines clearly.

One step removed from the basic work surface is the work table. This is a little larger and can be mounted onto screw-on legs. An old drawing board or something of similar size is ideal for this and even if it is no longer quite square the portable surface just described can be laid on it to provide this facility. Still truly portable, it has the advantage of providing that much more room to store all those items you wish you had thought of before you sat down! Two worthwhile additions can be made at little expense or effort. The first is a length of track, always handy for checking that you model will actually move without falling over. The second is a shallow container to hold all the bits and pieces that will roll off the edge at the slightest opportunity. It can also be used to hold those bottles of liquid adhesive which refuse to stick the kit together but will achieve instant and lasting adhesion with the lounge carpet, armchair or trouser leg.

Having constructed the work surface of your choice what are the minimum tools needed to make a start? First and foremost is a good quality craft knife and plenty of spare blades of various shapes. There are several good ones on the market and the choice is a matter of personal preference. Next in the order of priority is a good quality steel straight edge. The wooden or plastic school ruler is ideal for the purpose for which it was designed, that is, to measure. It is no good whatsoever as a cutting edge guide. Models are full of corners, most of them thankfully at 90°, so a small, say 4 in, engineer's set square is also valuable. Almost all model building problems begin in the very early stages of construction. Round things that are not quite round, or square things that are not quite square, will all compound the error as construction progresses. It is all but impossible to put right these errors at a late stage in construction when their collective effect really becomes apparent.

Half a dozen Swiss files will give easy access to all those odd corners and are particularly useful for opening out previously drilled holes or cleaning up small parts. Probably most useful are one each of; round fine, round coarse, flat fine, flat coarse, triangular fine and square fine. Not cheap tools, but properly looked after they will last for ever and will repay their first cost many times over. However they do not take kindly to being used as levers for opening paint tins!

Sooner or later you will have to start drilling holes in your models to attach handrails, handrail knobs and the like. Most of these holes will be of very small diameter and the actual drills correspondingly thin. In order not to place too big a load on the drill it is advisable to use a pin chuck. This can be turned between thumb and forefinger and can result in very accurate work. It is not necessary to buy a whole range of drills as it is always possible, indeed sometimes preferable, to drill a size smaller and open out with a round section Swiss file, especially if a force fit is required.

Another useful tool to acquire early is a scriber. It is ideal for marking out on plastic sheet and unlike pencil lines will not erase with subsequent handling. The addition of a couple of instrument screwdrivers, a pair of small pliers and a tin lid to keep bits and pieces in will form the basis of a good tool kit. It is certainly adequate for the successful construction of plastic kits and white metal 'body-line' kits which make use of a proprietary chassis.

Once your modelling is established further useful items can be added as listed below. Not only do they increase the range of modelling tasks that can be undertaken, they also make life that little bit more enjoyable. Small tools such as described here make ideal Christmas or birthday presents from the family and are much more fun to receive than socks and handkerchiefs. Although the initial cash outlay may appear to be expensive for physically small items this is not really so when compared to the price of more advanced kits. There is no point whatsoever in trying to build an £80 loco kit with a penknife and a couple of rusty old tools from the garage.

Basic tool kit
Work surface or work table
Steel straight edge 12 in long
Engineer's square
Craft knife with assorted blades
Swiss files — assorted
Pin chuck and selection of small drills
Instrument screwdrivers
Small pliers
Scriber
Bits tin

A good basic tool kit to begin with and not too expensive to purchase.

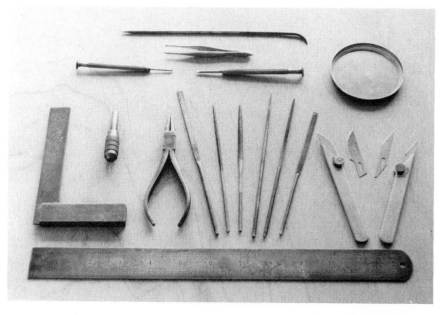

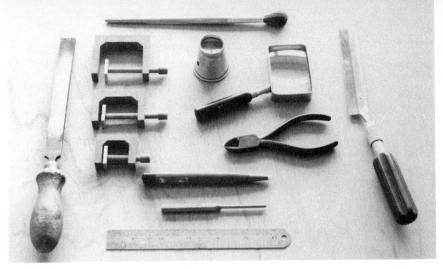

Useful additions to the basic tool kit, enabling a greater range of tasks to be undertaken.

Augmented tool kit
Basic tool kit
Magnifying glass or jeweller's eye glass
File, 6 in with safety edge
Razor saw
Glass fibre brush
Small clamps
Steel straight edge 6 in long
Soldering iron
Narrow nosed pliers
Tweezers
Wire cutters
'Romford' screwdriver
Test leads with small crocodile clips

Railway modelling is fun but you would do well to remember the following, first expounded by that well known Lancashire modeller Arkwright Sodd:

1 Any container that is full will be knocked over.
2 Paint tin lids always land paint side down.
3 Anything that is dropped will immediately assume the colour of its surroundings and vanish for ever.
4 Even if you are fortunate enough to see it go it will turn up eight feet away from where you know it fell.
5 Painted thumb prints will appear even when you have not painted anything for two weeks.
6 Your full requirements only become apparent one minute after the model shop closes on Saturday night.
7 Just when you are sitting comfortably, the phone rings.

Adhesives

These are readily available under various trade names but for simplicity will be described here in general terms.

Polystyrene tube cement

Not the best adhesive for assembling small models and prone to 'stringing'. It can be useful for reinforcing joints from the back, such as on buildings.

Polystyrene liquid cement

The ideal adhesive for plastic construction as it flows easily into all areas of the joint to be made. Simply applied by brush it can however creep in under fingers unnoticed, until you try to put the model down that is.

Super glue

A superb adhesive applied either directly from the tube or on the end of a cocktail stick. Gives a very strong and instant bond between two touching surfaces but will not fill in gaps in joints. Ideal for fixing small items with a minimum surface to surface contact. Gives off strong and irritant fumes.

Two part epoxy adhesive

Supplied in two tubes, neither of which is an adhesive by itself. The adhesive is formed by combining the two in equal amounts. Available with setting times between 5 minutes and 24 hours. Ideal for the heavier joints where strength is required.

Bostic type adhesive

Another tube adhesive, it is ideal for bonding dissimilar materials, for example, clear plastic glazing to a metal body. Quick acting but liable to 'stringing' so needs care.

Solder

I regret to record that I find myself totally unsuccessful in the use of the soldering iron. Talks with colleagues would seem to indicate that this is one of those methods that can either be used successfully or not at all. If the skill is given to you then it is by far the best way to assemble brass parts and white metal, remembering of course to use a low melting point solder in the latter case.

Modelling materials

Plastic

By far the easiest material to model in is plastic. It is reasonably cheap, easily obtained in various thicknesses or sections and produces very little waste. It can be cut, bent, filed or moulded and finished structures are light in weight. Where needed extra strength is easily obtained by lamination. Basic structures are easy to make including coach, wagon, and locomotive bodies but it will be necessary to make provision for the addition of ballast.

Card

Another easily obtainable material with all of the same qualities and uses as plastic card, but with one disadvantage. Most cards will require to be sealed with varnish to prevent them absorbing water and consequently warping. Large structures such as buildings may also need to be well braced.

Sheet metal

The most commonly used of these is brass or nickel silver. More expensive in first cost, the finished article is much stronger, reasonable in weight and less prone to accidental damage.

Safety

It may seem that railway modelling is just about as safe a hobby as it is possible to practise. However, it does use a number of materials that give off fumes and employs quite a range of sharp tools. It makes sense then to follow the manufacturers' instructions and keep paints, adhesives and tools out of the reach of small children. Never smoke while using liquid plastic adhesive to avoid inhaling fumes.

Two other lessons learned, fortunately from the experience of others. Never, never put a mains type plug onto a lead unless it is intended to carry that voltage. Mains voltage across a 12 volt motor produces about a million scale horse power at the draw-bar for a couple of micro-seconds and does it no good at all. It also makes the track potentially lethal. You may know that that particular plug does not go into the mains socket but someone else, a child for instance, may not.

Lastly, when making small items by home casting do not use Polyfilla or any other plaster type material as a mould. All of these materials attract water out of the atmosphere so that when hot metal is poured into them this water converts instantly into steam. The resulting explosion you will not believe and an ounce or so of molten metal can achieve damage difficult to comprehend unless you have seen it.

Chapter 10

Painting and lining

There is no doubt that some modellers have an in-built ability to paint, line and letter their models to an enviable standard. It is also true that many more could achieve a high standard given a few guidelines as to the way to go about it.

To begin with it is necessary to accept that a first class finish is the result of patience, care and not a little pre-planning. There is nothing magical about it and the series of guidelines given here are the result of hard won experience.

Paints

It is safe to say that amongst the well known brands there is no such thing as a bad paint on the market although their ease of application and drying times may vary considerably. It is necessary to experiment and find a range that suits the individual.

Generally speaking all paint is too thick for satisfactory application as it is supplied. It is equally true that few tins are full to the very top so there is adequate room for the addition of thinners. How much to thin is a question often asked. Many years ago the author was fortunate enough to be able to discuss the question of paint finishes on models with the late Mr Ross Pochin, he of Furness Railway fame and the builder and painter of many superb models. His advice was to take a tin of, say, Humbrol paint, add white spirit, stir, and keep on adding small amounts of white spirit until you are convinced it is overdone — and then add just a little bit more. It will then be just about right. A bit rudimentary you might say, but it certainly works and the standard of painting on his own models left no doubt. In practice thin and test as you go along. At the correct consistency the paint should flow easily off your stirring implement in steady drops. Practice will soon teach the correct proportions. For a really first class finish it will be necessary to apply a number of coats, maybe as many as six or seven. The end result will, however, be worth it. If anyone tells you that their model was painted with only one coat it will be possible to reply in all honesty that you can tell.

At the end of this thinning process, if you find that you have overdone it recovery is still possible by leaving the lid off the tin and allowing the excess thinners to evaporate. Remember too that if you are painting in a centrally heated room or on a warm summer's day the thinners will evaporate that much more quickly and a lengthy job may well require the addition of a little more thinners half way through.

All paint manufacturers will tell you that their products must be mixed

Class A4 Liveries 1.

Livery carried by first A4, 2509 Silver Link.
Smokebox front — dark charcoal.
Side skirting and frames — battleship grey.
Cab roof between rainstrips — dark charcoal.
Engine, cab, tender body and all wheels including tender — silver grey.
Silver lettering shaded blue. Name plate on casing.
Note   The locomotive left the plant in this scheme, but was altered at front end before entering traffic.

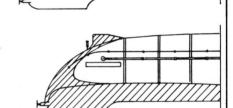

2509, 2510, 2511 and 2512.
Main colour scheme as above but charcoal grey now formed parabolic curve. Nameplates removed and name painted onto side in silver, shaded blue.

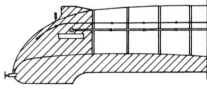

4482, 4493, 4494 and 4495.
Above painted initially in variation of standard lined green scheme. Smokebox and side skirting painted black.

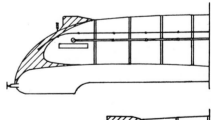

Class A4 Liveries 2.

4483, 4484, 4485, 4486 and 4487.
Black paint carried back to first boiler band. This did little to enhance the streamlined shape.

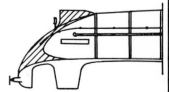

All locomotives
Standard garter blue and black scheme with either transfers or stainless steel lettering and trim. All replaced by plain black during World War 2. Division of black/blue marked by red and blue line $1/4$ in wide — red leading.

Post-war garter blue scheme, but note side valances removed. Double chimney only fitted to 4468, 4901, 4902 and 4903 when built. Others acquired double chimneys under BR ownership.

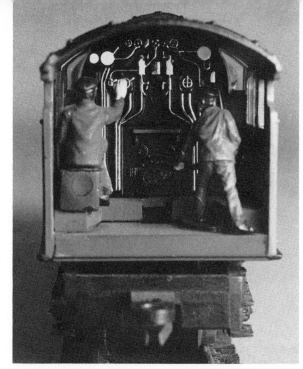

Simple modifications can be worthwhile. Dials picked out in white and the addition of a crew lend more interest.

thoroughly prior to use. This does not mean half a dozen quick twiddles with a match stick! To save time and also really mix the paint the following method can be used. Before doing anything select the tin or tins of paint to be used and check their consistency. New tins or those that have been standing for some time may have all of the pigment settled on the bottom. In this case carry out an initial stir until it is all in suspension, even if still lumpy. Replace the lid firmly and hold in the hand and shake continuously whilst collecting the many bits and pieces needed for your work. By the time you are ready to start, the shaking action and the heat of your hand will ensure that the paint is well and truly ready for use.

Brushes

The old saying of 'you never get owt for nowt' is particularly true when applied to brushes. Cheap brushes are just that and will produce a poor finish and frustration in just about equal amounts. For most model painting it is not necessary to have a vast selection of brushes, therefore buy the best you can afford and treat them as you would any other tool. Be aware that the nearer a model comes to completion the harder it gets to recover from a disaster. For this reason it is recommended that at least two brushes be kept for specific tasks. The first of these should be a brush with a large head on it. This is used exclusively for dusting off models prior to painting. The long hairs will get into all the corners without knocking off detail items. The second is kept specifically for varnishing. Never use them for anything else, if necessary colour code the handles so that they do not get used by mistake. All brushes should be cleaned thoroughly immediately after use, which does not mean a quick wiggle in an almost-black jar of thinners! Clean thinner should be kept for thinning paint, another lot for final brush cleaning and a used lot for initial cleaning. This is not quite as wasteful as it might seem as only lot two will need to be replaced as lot three becomes unusable.

Painting a model

Preparation

It could be argued that this is the most important of all the steps in painting. Old solder, adhesive, or a great greasy thumb print may not be all that obvious until the paint goes on, but after that they will show horribly and will be impossible to clean off or hide. Generally the cleaning process is quick and easy. For metal models a wash over with methylated spirits will remove grease effectively and for plastic models a good scrub in warm soapy water will suffice. An old toothbrush is ideal for this, but beware of rubbing too hard and knocking off the detail work. Rinse in warm clear water and then leave to dry thoroughly in the air. Make sure that no water is trapped in such places as cab corners or where the boiler joins the footplate.

When the model is clean and dry apply a thin coat of light grey matt paint all over. (For brass or other metal models a self-etch primer should be used first, this helps to key the paint to the metal surface.) When the paint is dry have a good long hard look at your model and you may be surprised at just how many knife or file marks you can see. Now is the time to rub down these areas and if the problem is really pronounced it may be advisable to recoat with grey again just to make sure. This initial coat must be quite thin as any brush marks left on the model at this stage will still be visible under the top coats and the final varnish.

Painting sequence

Always paint to a plan remembering that somehow you will have to hold the model, turn it over, and turn it round. A little thought here will ensure that you will always have an area to hold. Work logically along a boiler or tender side. Do not apply too much at one go and never be tempted to go back over an area whilst it is still wet. Beware too of the brush that is shedding hairs. These are all but invisible when the paint is going on, but look like a tree trunk when the paint is dry. If you do see a stray hair lift it away with the very tip of a nearly dry brush and then leave it alone. Any minor damage done can be put right next time around. Apply repeated coats of paint until you are satisfied that the required density has been achieved. As a rough guide, and assuming the paint has been thinned as described, three coats of green will be sufficient for a plastic body moulded in green, but where the original colour was black six or seven coats may be needed although this number can be markedly reduced if a grey base coat has been put on first. Wagon grey is particularly good at 'killing' original colours, especially red.

Most proprietary model railway paints dry with a matt or semi-matt finish. When it comes to applying transfers or rub down lettering, numbering or lining, it is better done on a shiny surface. To achieve this apply two coats of gloss varnish also well thinned down. When the first coat has dried look at it and it will give you

Above The GNR eight-wheeled tender built to the drawings shown, and detailed. Basically a plastic box, it is a simple conversion. *Below left* Close-up view of the front of the GNR pattern eight-wheeled tender. A bit basic regarding detail, but when it was built photographs were hard to come by. *Below Right* Rear view of the same tender. The coal rails, notoriously fragile on a model of this size, are solid with the detail painted on.

the fright of your life. What has happened is that it will have soaked into the matt paint and will exhibit a very uneven finish. Not to worry, this is normal and successive coats will bring up the gloss and result in a first class finish. When all the numbering, lining or lettering has been applied a top coat of varnish will give a most satisfactory finish. It is also a good idea to put an extra coat of varnish onto those areas which are often handled such as footplate edges. If a high gloss finish is not required then the final coat of varnish should be matt or satin finish.

Weathering

This is the term used to describe a paint finish representing a locomotive or vehicle that has been some time in traffic. Before going further it should be appreciated that for much of the life of the LNER, and many other railways too, locomotives were cleaned on a regular basis by shed staff. Additional cleaning might also be carried out by the crew so that, except in wartime, the truly filthy locomotive was not an everyday sight. There is a world of difference between a traffic stained finish and that sometimes offered up as weathering, if the latter was scaled up the muck would be 4 in thick in some cases!

Before attempting to weather a locomotive or piece of rolling stock two things need to be done. First of all, find a good photograph of the chosen subject in everyday use. Secondly, try to imagine your choice in normal use. Where are the stains and patches of discoloration most likely to occur? Which areas are going to be difficult for the shed staff or crew to reach and therefore least likely to be cleaned regularly? Boiler and firebox tops, cab, coach or van roofs are obvious candidates. Anywhere on the locomotive where there is jointed pipework can and

A reasonably clean, but work-stained, Class D34 'Glen'. Note the staining on tender and boiler. A GEM white metal body and tender kit on a Hornby 4-4-0 chassis. Note the small style of lettering on the tender.

probably does leak so that staining would occur from safety valves, around the dome, snifting valves etc. A burnt smokebox door might also be evident caused by a less than airtight joint allowing air to be sucked in and causing the contents, and the door in extreme cases, to glow red hot. Steam locomotives used vast quantities of water and even a humble shunter might have to replenish its supply several times in a spell of duty. This operation too left its mark, either as a clean patch on good paintwork or as a rust streaked stain where paint was poor. All of this can be represented in model form with a little bit of care and imagination.

Painting 'teak'

To avoid confusion it must be appreciated that the word 'teak' has two distinct applications when used to describe the finish of the majority of LNER coaching stock. In the first case it applies to paint straight out of a tin and applied to solebars, headstocks, buffer housings and wheel centres. Painting these is a straightforward operation taking the same precautions and using the same methods as for locomotive painting.

The teak grained finish is another matter entirely, even if the ingredients do come out of a tin, or rather a number of tins. What is being attempted is the representation of a natural wood grain finish in a scale far below full size and without actually using any wood, it is therefore an art finish. It is this difference in scale that makes the use of wood veneers so impracticable in all but the very largest of models. It is also a sad fact that many otherwise good models of teak stock have been ruined by being finished in what looks like the results of a collision with a train load of cocoa! Sad because it is entirely unnecessary.

If the model to be grained is scratch or kit built then preparation is simple and

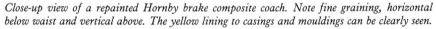

Close-up view of a repainted Hornby brake composite coach. Note fine graining, horizontal below waist and vertical above. The yellow lining to casings and mouldings can be clearly seen.

only normal pre-cleaning need be carried out. If however a previously painted model is to be used then all lettering, numbering and lining will first have to be removed. To illustrate this the method is described for painting a Hornby LNER coach.

In many ways this is an ideal vehicle as a first exercise. True, it is not exactly a scale vehicle, making many concessions to the toy train market, being too high, too short, devoid of some characteristically LNER detail and containing other detail which has nothing to do with the LNER. However all the essential style of panelling and beading is there and they can quite often be picked up cheaply second-hand. It is also possible to carry out some simple modifications during the painting task which will visibly improve the finished article. For the purpose of illustration the vehicle in question is a five compartment corridor brake third/first composite, Hornby catalogue number R436. The method will apply to any vehicle of this type, including the excellent Ian Kirk coach kits in his LNER range.

1 Pull out bogies and spring out wheels — set aside.
2 Squeeze together retaining lugs at end of body and remove floor, underframe, seat and glazing unit as one.
3 Squeeze inwards retaining lugs of glazing unit and remove. This releases the seat unit and will reveal the metal weight underneath. Slide off the coach ends and set aside. Note that the floor, seat and glazing units are all marked with a star at one end. This ensures that everything is replaced the correct way round. This completes the stripping operation.
4 Fill a basin with warm water and add a drop or two of washing up liquid. Put all component parts into this and scrub off with an old toothbrush. Be careful not to apply too much pressure on the glazing unit or this will crack across its length. On some examples of this model the washing operation will also remove the transfers. On others it will be necessary to use a cloth dipped in white spirit. Never use an abrasive unless you enjoy spending hours rubbing down afterwards.
5 Paint one coat of gloss yellow onto all exterior bodywork panelling, including the end panels.
6 Paint one coat of gloss yellow onto all of the 'timber' sections of the seating unit including the inner and outer faces of the corridor partition.
7 Take the glazing unit and lay it down with the painted handrails on the bench side. Using a scriber make a small indent into the plastic at the outer ends of each handrail. This will align the replacement handrails in the correct place. Use a mild polish such as Duraglit until all trace of the painted handrails is removed. Polish off, rinse and let dry. When dry thoroughly polish all over, finish with a soft cloth and from then on handle only by the ends.
8 Paint the solebars, headstocks and buffer housings with Compucolor LNER teak. This is as close as you will get to the real colour.
9 Make a decision on wheels. As moulded the bogies will take 14 mm coach disc wheels as manufactured by Maygib or the originals can be used. Paint the centres teak and the wheel rims white. When dry spring back into the

bogie side frames and set aside.

10 Paint the upholstery in the appropriate colour, not forgetting the matching carpet in first class compartments and corridors.

11 From brass wire make up suitable lengths to represent corridor handrails and fix from behind with fast setting epoxy resin adhesive as per the diagram. Paint the windows of toilet compartments white, including the one left clear on the original.

12 Before applying the main teak finish paint the inner edges of all windows, both on the body and the corridor partition, with Precision Paints LNER teak.

13 Using Precision Paints LNER teak paint, apply graining affect to body and end panels. Experience has shown that this is the best paint to achieve the grained effect. Pay particular attention to the direction of the grain. On the coach side all graining is horizontal below waist level and vertical above to cantrail level. The cantrail is also teak. All the graining on the coach end is vertical. Grain each panel individually, starting at one end with a lightly loaded brush and work steadily, brushing out to the panel end. Pick up the door frames as you go and once again never go back and try to touch up with the paint still wet. The aim is to suggest a timber effect rather than produce an obviously wooden finish, after all the model is many times reduced from full size. Aim to portray a fine grain effect on all panels and to match the shading as you go. Repeat the exercise for the partition walls and the corridor partition. In this case all graining is vertical. When the teak paint is dry it will all look very drab and uninspiring. However when clear varnished it will come up nicely and show a beautiful colour.

14 Next apply all lettering, numbering and lining and a further coat of varnish. Set aside to dry under a dust cover.

15 Now reassemble the vehicle in the reverse order to stripping, making sure that any stray finger marks have been cleaned off the glazing. This done, apply the final coat of varnish.

16 Attention can now be turned to the roof which is painted overall matt white, including the portion moulded into the coach ends.

17 One further modification remains to be made and is well worth doing. As supplied, the coach has a corridor connecting door to a design not remotely connected with the LNER. Cut out a blank of plastic card as an insert for the non-brake end, teak grain, varnish and fit. Paint the outside of the corridor connection matt black and the inside edges cream. At the brake end cut out a plastic card blank to go over the corridor connection, fit, and paint matt black. Add a tail lamp and the vehicle is ready to return to service.

Lining

Of all model painting tasks this is the most difficult and is also the most obvious if done badly. It makes no sense to do it the hard way, so if a proprietary brand exists, use it. Again this is where painting and lining to a plan will pay dividends.

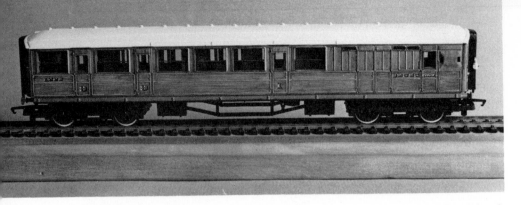

The Hornby five compartment brake composite after a visit to the paintshop, illustrating the modifications described.

For example, in most cases it will be advantageous to leave off boiler, cab and tender handrails until all lining is completed.

Where no suitable lining is available it is necessary to resort to hand lining. This is not as difficult as it may first appear and practice makes perfect. Some lining may be better done by fine brush and size 000 is very useful for this task. Other lining can be done using a draughtsman's lining pen. This is particularly useful when lining mouldings and casings on coaching stock. It is most important that paint used for this lining is well thinned so that it flows more like an ink.

Screw the legs of the pen together so that the points just touch. Using a brush, load the pen with a quantity of paint. For a reasonably sized job about 1/8 of an inch will do. Any more and the pen will flood. Make sure that no paint has found its way onto the outside of the pen as this will cause the whole thing to discharge as soon as you put pen to model. The angle at which the pen meets the surface to be lined will vary according to the type of surface. On a tender side, for example, it should be held at an angle normally used with any other type of pen and drawn along the straight edge in one steady movement. If the flow of paint should cause a break in the line do not attempt to go over it again until the paint is dry. All that will happen is that the line already there will be destroyed. Before drawing any line on a model the line thickness and the paint flow should always be tested on a piece of scrap and adjustments made before lining proper.

The technique for lining casings and mouldings is exactly the same up until the pen is applied to the model. In this case a much flatter angle is adopted. There is no need to try and do a delicate balancing operation of keeping the point of the pen exactly on top of the raised moulding. In fact the line can be drawn from the side of the pen towards the very tip and will provide a thin line of uniform thickness. This lining operation does not lend itself to the use of any aid such as a straight edge but again practice makes for confidence. Watch the consistency of the paint and thin as required and always clean the pen, especially at the tip, between each loading.

It may be that there will be odd corners which the pen will not be able to get into. In that case the size 000 brush can be used to touch in the missing area. When satisfied with the job always protect the lining with a coat of varnish.

Chapter 11

Practical modelling

Many years ago, when railway modelling was in its infancy, there grew up a breed of modeller who was adept at turning his hand to almost any task. Give him a supply of empty cocoa tins and a soldering iron and the most marvellous models would result. This had to be so, as very little variety was available from a somewhat limited trade. A comparison of model railway magazines then and now will show just how far the hobby has progressed in the intervening years. In those days a model layout was classed as 'scenic' if it boasted a station, signal box and maybe an advertising hoarding or two. Any modeller today who tried to get away with that would be laughed out of court. In many areas the modeller has never been so well served as he is now with the trade providing many items either as ready to use or as kits. Unfortunately this has led to a loss of the inventive spirit and, sad to say, there are many who if it doesn't come out of a box are completely stumped. However it does not need to be like that and a bit of thought, not to mention lateral thinking, will produce wonders. In a number of cases the answer to the problem can be provided subject to a little bit of applied ingenuity. Some useful hints and tips follow to enable the railway modeller of today to recapture some of the expertise and ingenuity of modellers past.

Making parallel boilers
This is, without doubt, the heart of a good model locomotive. If this feature is incorrect then everything else looks wrong too. The most obvious solution is to acquire a piece of brass tubing of the correct diameter and work up from there. This generally means work with a soldering iron to affix detail work and may be beyond the modeller's skill or range of equipment. It can also be a fairly expensive solution and the material itself difficult to come by in exactly the right size. For an inexpensive solution plastic sheet is an ideal raw material which is relatively cheap, easy to obtain and as a material is both easy to work and forgiving of mistakes. How then do you make a boiler out of flat plastic card?

To begin with it is necessary to mark out accurately the length of the boiler, remembering to allow for the firebox assembly to protrude into the cab. It can also be desirable for overall strength to allow for the length of the smokebox in the initial construction and add the smokebox itself as an additional wrapper. The circumference of the boiler need not be calculated so accurately, provided that any error is on the side of excess, as this can always be cut away later. What is needed is some simple method to convert flat sheet into a boiler with a truly round cross-

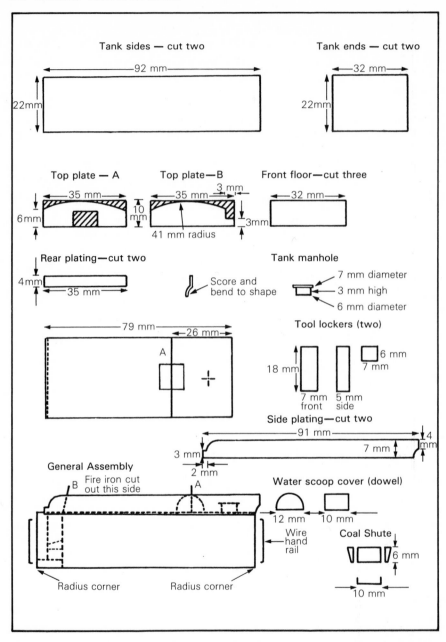

Drawing of parts needed to construct a simple GNR pattern eight-wheeled tender body in 4mm scale. Designed to fit on to the Hornby tender chassis.

section and, more importantly, a circular section that is not naturally always trying to return itself to a flat sheet. The first item to obtain is a piece of close grained timber, say 4 in by 4 in by $\frac{1}{2}$ in. This forms the base of the boiler maker and makes it safe to handle at a later stage. Next acquire a light alloy tube of the kind used to package denture cleaning tablets. These generally come in two lengths and for this purpose the smaller of the two will do. Drill a hole in the bottom of the tube and a corresponding hole in the centre of the piece of timber. Pass a threaded screw down through the tube and fasten with a nut to the bottom of the timber base. Allow a recess so that the screw and nut leave the base unobstructed so that it sits level (see diagram). Having cut the piece of plastic, roll it into a roughly circular shape in water as hot as you can bear by rolling it around a length of dowel. Now ease this roughly formed shape into the tube and push down firmly so that the lower end is seated absolutely square. Place the device on a suitable surface, the draining board will do, and pour boiling water into the tube. This causes two reactions, firstly it makes the material pliable and secondly it expands evenly to the inside diameter of the tube. Pick the whole lot up by the base and run cold tap water into the tube until it is cold. This returns the material to a rigid state and also removes any inherent stress. Remove the plastic from the tube and there is your basic boiler. It can now be offered up to the drawing and the excess in the diameter marked on one edge of the tube. This can now be trimmed away, best

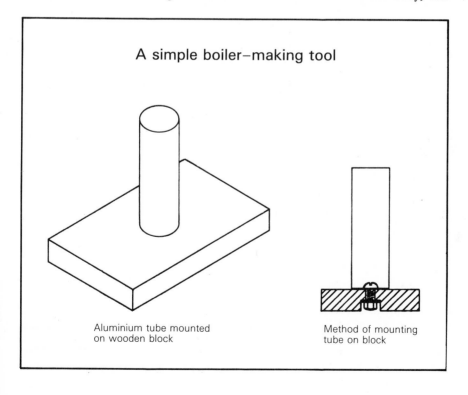

A simple boiler–making tool

Aluminium tube mounted
on wooden block

Method of mounting
tube on block

done a little at a time and with frequent reference to the drawing, until the correct diameter is achieved. Smooth off the joining edges and tape with Sellotape to hold in position. Mark off the position of boiler bands and fix with liquid cement making sure that the joint on these is not coincident with the joint on the boiler. Leave to set hard and then run liquid cement along the boiler joint. This will produce a rigid unit which will make no attempt to return to its original shape. If the model requires some of the underside of the boiler to be cut away to accommodate a motor then leave this operation until last. Similarly make a smokebox wrapper and fit around the front of the boiler unit, sticking with liquid cement. The boiler is now ready for mounting on the frames and to have its fittings added.

Making tapered boilers

The principle involved is exactly the same as that used for the parallel boiler but on this occasion it is necessary to make an additional jig. This consists of two circular discs cut to the outside diameter of the boiler at both ends of the taper less *twice* the thickness of the plastic sheet to be used. These should be mounted the correct distance apart on a rigid beam, thick plastic or plastic tube will do. In this case the plastic sheet should be cut over length, but still square, and then moulded into a circular cross-section as described above. The finished tube should then be eased over the discs and positioned so that they are enclosed completely at each

Three white metal kits in the course of construction. Tank locos like these were the workhorses of the railway and gave yeoman service, if largely unrecognized. They are useful models for a layout as they are so versatile.

end. It is then a simple matter to run a soft pencil around the inside edge and trim to length. The finished shape can then be cemented to its own bulkheads and completion is as already described. With plastic sheet and boiling water it is possible to overcome many of the problems associated with boiler making and, being a cheap method, if the first effort is not quite right it is not a disaster.

Templates

'If you are going to make more than two of anything, make a template first, it will save you hours of work in the long run.' This piece of advice was given to me many years ago and has stood the test of time. Any templates made are effectively part of the tool kit and as such are likely to come in for some rough handling so that this is one case where brass or nickel silver sheet can be used to advantage. There are many uses for templates and it is essential that when made they are made accurately. Any error in the original will be produced in every subsequent piece and will require corrective action, a really tedious and unnecessary process. Depending upon what is being made the modeller will quickly discover his own need for templates so that only a few examples are given here of simple applications.

One obvious application is in marking off and preparing plastic compartment partitions for use in Ian Kirk non-corridor coach kits. The parts supplied in the kit are adequate but a far better job can be done by making new ones that follow the inside curvature of the roof. Another application on coaching stock is for the inner blanks on the vestibule connectors on the Hornby LNER coaches or the outer blanks on brake ended vehicles. Similarly the two Class B12 conversions described earlier benefited from having the new cab sides marked out from a master template. Another useful template can be made out of a piece of brass or aluminium angle. Marked left and right handed, they are used to position both transfer letters and plastic 'stainless steel' letters on the sides of eight-wheeled tenders. This automatically ensures that the line of letters is correctly spaced and level with the tender base. Useful tools all, and well worth taking the time out to make.

Casting

It is almost certain that at some stage in your model making you will require a part that nobody makes. This is particularly true when carrying out conversions of existing models. Probably not more than one or two specialized bits are required so it is easier if these can be made in the home workshop. To begin with it will be necessary to make a master from which all castings will be made. Depending upon what the item is will depend the material from which the master is made. Illustrated is a Hornby Class A4 converted to a single chimney from the double version with which the model is supplied by means of a casting. A necessary operation if anything other than the four double chimney A4s is to be portrayed. To begin with a number of layers of plastic sheet were cemented together and, when thoroughly dry, carved and sanded to shape. The master was then drilled slightly undersized to take a brass screw about half an inch long. The reason for

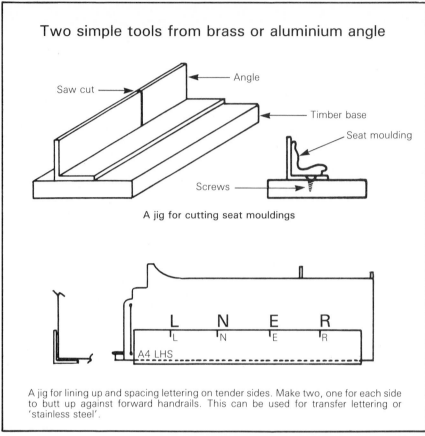

Two simple tools from brass or aluminium angle

A jig for cutting seat mouldings

A jig for lining up and spacing lettering on tender sides. Make two, one for each side to butt up against forward handrails. This can be used for transfer lettering or 'stainless steel'.

A modified Hornby Class A4, Kingfisher. *The original double chimney has been replaced by the single variety cast in the home workshop. British Rail number and shed plates have been removed, lamps fitted and 'stainless steel' lettering and numbers added from thinned down plastic letters.*

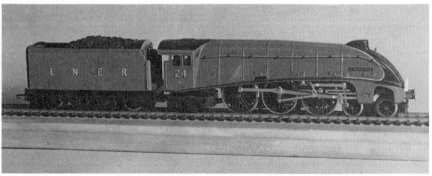

this is simply so that it can be handled more easily. The material in which to make the casting was found by trial and error but eventually Loctite Handy Strip proved to be satisfactory. This is moulded in the fingers into a roughly cubic shape and then pressed onto a thin piece of ply. Before it set the master was coated with a thin layer of cycle oil and pressed firmly in. The oil prevents the master from sticking to the mould and distorting it upon withdrawal and can easily be washed off afterwards. A small quantity of low melting point metal was heated until liquid and then carefully poured into the mould. The first two were quite successful in shape but had a large bulge on their undersides caused by surface tension. This was going to be a nuisance but the problem was solved accidently. The third casting was over filled by mistake and as the metal overflowed the bulge simply disappeared to leave a nice flat base. The excess metal is easy to break away and can go back into the melting pot. Once cool, which does not take long, the casting is easy to remove from the mould, having shrunk slightly. A quick clean up will produce a nice chimney and if any are not satisfactory they can be melted down and recast.

Cutting and turning

One useful source of boiler fittings can be found amongst those already available as spares from various suppliers, even though they are not exactly the shape that is required. What is needed is one that is almost correct but with enough metal in it to allow for reduction and reshaping all round. Spare chimneys and domes are available in a variety of shapes and are variously made of turned brass, as brass lost wax castings or as white metal castings. The turned brass version will normally have a hole right through it whereas most castings do not. However it is a simple matter to drill them out which is an essential first step before turning can commence. This completed, an old paint brush handle is used as a mandrel and the casting forced tightly on to it. Now place the handle into the chuck of a hand drill, turn the handle and you have an instant lathe. It might seem crude but it is a very cheap method and it works.

The fitting can then be turned down or reshaped using various needle files. The chimney fitted to the plastic bodied Class C16 illustrated was shaped in this way, having begun life as a brass parallel sided GWR chimney. Although it was possible to obtain the taper required it remained a fraction too tall. The only way to reduce the height was to cut right through it and fix the top back on. The problem was how to cut at the correct angle so that the two parts could be rejoined so that they were square and parallel. The answer again turned out to be simple. Scribe a line lightly down the length of the chimney, saw it through as carefully as possible, clean up with files and join. As long as the two parts are joined so that the scribed line is continuous then any error in the cutting will be cancelled because it will be constant on both halves.

Other small fittings such as safety valves, whistles and snifting valves can be turned up out of brass rod using the drill and file method. Domes are best filed to shape by hand but if they have to be reduced in height by cutting then the scribed line method will again ensure that the finished article is square.

Mixing materials

As mentioned previously it is possible for the LNER modeller to increase the number and types of models available to him by carrying out detailed conversions. This applies equally well to ready to run models or to kits. Two such modifications are illustrated in this book, one being the Class J39 to J38 conversion and the other the Class D11/1 to D11/2. In the first case it was necessary to remove the splashers from the footplate casting and this resulted in the space for the wheels becoming visible as rectangular gaps. These needed to be disguised and this was done by cutting a piece of thin plastic card to the overall shape of the footplate casting and gluing it over the top. A thin layer of Bostik Clear adhesive was applied to both surfaces and then they were gently but firmly pressed together. When set they were trimmed off and the rest of the kit assembled as per the instructions. Thin brass sheet could have been used but none of the correct thickness was available at the time. In any case previous experience had shown that provided both materials to be joined were thoroughly clean they would stick together satisfactorily. It was also highly unlikely that any problems would be encountered with the different rates of expansion of the two materials as the amounts involved were not large. This had already been proved when the Class D11/2 had been modified.

In this case the original kit had one serious error, serious in that it completely spoiled the visual effect. This concerned the vertical height of the driving wheel splashers which were far too shallow. It was cured by building up the height, again using plastic card and carrying this over the leading edge curve. After being allowed to set thoroughly it was filed and sanded to shape and the locomotive has since given many years of service without any sign of movement between the two materials.

From the few foregoing examples it will be seen that much can be accomplished in the home workshop without the need for complicated or expensive devices. Practice also makes perfect, so if the first attempt does not come up to expectations go back and try again. It really is surprising how often the answer to a problem will suddenly present itself, so do not give up just because the item needed cannot be bought over the shop counter.

Two small layouts

Not the least of the problems to be solved by the railway modeller is what sort of layout to build. This decision is, more often than not, influenced by the space, time and money available. Illustrated here are plans for two small layouts that were built for home and exhibition use. In these cases size was influenced not by space restrictions in the home but by the fact that the baseboard had to be transported in a Volkswagen Beetle, not a vehicle renowned for its spacious interior. A baseboard 6 ft by 1 ft 6 in would go in, just, together with the stand, the stock, and the driver. Neither layout was based upon a prototype but was designed as a moving showcase for models of LNER locomotives. With both layouts the emphasis was on keeping something on show and also something moving at all times. To judge from public reaction the visitors found these attractive and they

Layout A.

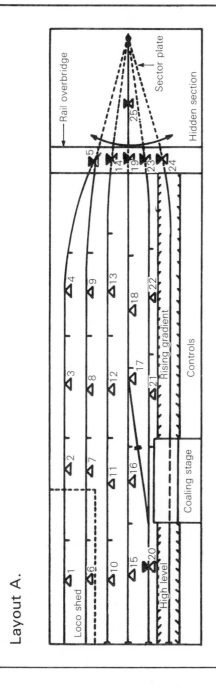

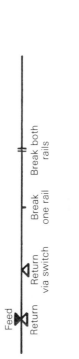

This layout measures 6 ft by 1 ft 6 in and is constructed on 2 in by 1 in framing. Designed for exhibition use, it also makes an interesting layout for home use. The seven feeds and 25 returns, each of the latter through an ON/OFF switch, involve quite a bit of simple wiring but provide great versatility in use. The length of each section will depend upon the types of locomotives it is intended to use.

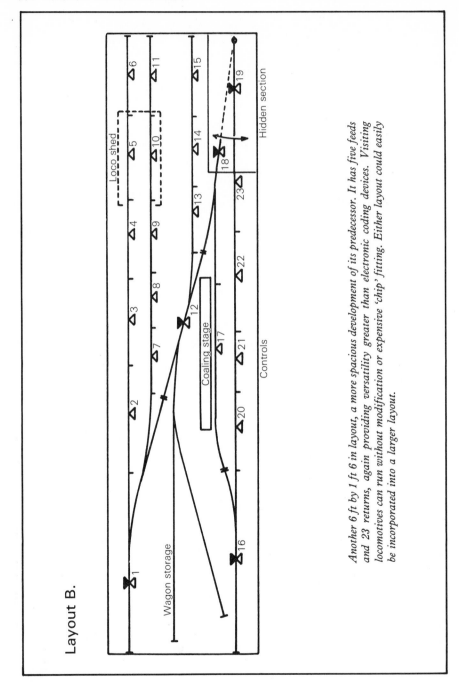

Layout B.

Another 6 ft by 1 ft 6 in layout, a more spacious development of its predecessor. It has five feeds and 23 returns, again providing versatility greater than electronic coding devices. Visiting locomotives can run without modification or expensive 'chip' fitting. Either layout could easily be incorporated into a larger layout.

were fun to operate. Both are capable of supporting many more locomotives than are actually on display at any one time. It was also interesting to note signs of barely concealed domestic conflict. More than one lady, on stopping to view, was heard to say, 'Now then, if you had something like that'!

Baseboard construction is quite straightforward, consisting of screwing a piece of Contiboard to 2 in by 1 in timber frame. Cork underlay $\frac{1}{8}$ in thick was used under the visible running tracks. This thickness was chosen because it vastly reduces the noise level and it is compatible in thickness with the hardboard used for the sector plate.

Layout A

As will be seen from the drawing this layout was designed to provide as much track as possible and yet retain the ability to represent railway operations and features. The high level coaling stage was one such as was the locomotive shed. All tracks, including that from the incline serving the coaling stage, passed under a bridge and on to the sector plate. The area was covered over and used as a static display. This design of layout could accommodate eighteen locomotives and still leave room for movement.

Layout B

This layout incorporated many of the ideas from layout A but attempted to depict a more open and railway-like atmosphere. The track plan employed more pointwork and not all trackwork was used for the storage of locomotives. The two unsectioned tracks at the left hand end for example were used to store loco coal wagons, tool and mess vans etc as well as an ash removal area. This layout could accommodate seventeen locomotives with room to operate.

Wiring

The wiring is simplicity itself and operates on the normal two-rail system of feed and return. On layout A there are 25 feeds and seven returns and on layout B there are 23 feeds and five returns. Each section is controlled by an on–off switch in the feed wiring, the whole being collectively mounted on a panel attached to one edge of the baseboard. A small track diagram was also shown on this panel and all switches were numbered. In practice locomotive movements called for the selection of switches in batches so that it was not too difficult to learn the sequence required. The length of each section of track was governed by the overall length of the locomotive that it was intended to store. Some would hold a Pacific whilst others were designed specifically for use with small tank locomotives or tender designs. Each cut rail was lined up and held by a shortened Peco rail joiner of the insulated type. At first glance layouts such as these would seem to be ideal for use with the Hornby Zero One System. However, the cost of installation and microchips could easily pay for two or three more second-hand locomotives. The choice is yours.

Sector plate

This very simple device can be made in a very short time and saves on turnouts as well as space. Use a piece of hardboard of the faced kind often used for panelling on kitchen units. Drill for and fix a pivot at one end. Also drill two small holes in the baseboard at the pivot end. These should be positioned outside of the

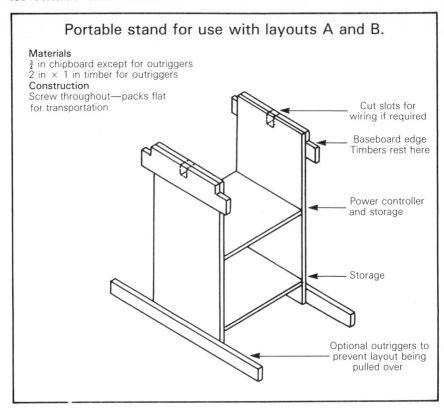

Portable stand for use with layouts A and B.

Materials
¾ in chipboard except for outriggers
2 in × 1 in timber for outriggers
Construction
Screw throughout—packs flat
for transportation

Cut slots for
wiring if required

Baseboard edge
Timbers rest here

Power controller
and storage

Storage

Optional outriggers to
prevent layout being
pulled over

maximum limit of travel of the sector plate and immediately opposite the pivot. This position puts the least strain upon the wires that both feed to and return from this piece of track. A piece of plain track is then stuck down to the sector plate along a marked centreline and the wiring soldered to it. Where the wiring comes up through the baseboard allow a generous amount to absorb movement and tie a knot in it to stop it being pulled back through the hole. A smear of furniture polish between the baseboard top and the underside of the sector plate will make for really free movement. It was never found necessary to provide any stops at each track end as correct lining up could easily be achieved with practice.

The convenience of a layout such as those depicted here is self evident. The fact that they do not take too long to build, require minimal maintenance and are fun to operate, even if they are restricted in the main to locomotives, is all to the modeller's advantage. Not quite so necessary in the home but an absolute must for exhibition work is the provision of a good robust stand for the layout. Those shown sat on top of a central pedestal which as well as giving support also provided storage for the controller and all those boxes that seem to accumulate. The sight of a layout crashing to the floor during an exhibition is not one to be forgotten and the damage that can ensue is both tragic and unnecessary.

Conclusion

Finally, a word to the newcomer to the hobby, based upon personal experience and from many hours spent helping out behind the counter of a model shop. Railway modelling is fun and it is also a hobby which is progressive. Start with something simple in the way of a layout and certainly when building your first locomotive. Large layouts are time consuming to build, expensive and require a lot of maintenance to keep them running properly.

On the locomotive side there are one or two nice body-line kits on the market that fit simply onto proprietary chassis. These are ideal for those wishing to make a move beyond ready to run stock and will teach you a lot about techniques and the handling of different materials. It may well be that you really want to build a Pacific but do resist the temptation to start off with this as a first project. There is

The modified rear end of the tender for Sir Visto, *showing alterations to original corridor tender. A simple job using plastic sheet.*

nothing sadder than the face of a modeller who presents himself complete with box and begins by saying, 'I wonder if you can help me?' He then produces a half finished model with just about everything wrong with it including one or two home grown modifications thrown in for good measure. If one were being totally honest the kindest advice would be to throw the kit away and find something useful to do with the box. More often than not it means completely stripping the locomotive to its component parts and starting again. Whilst the principle of construction of a white metal kit is very similar to that used with plastic kits the amount of preparation is not. Plastic kits in the main require little cleaning up and go together exactly as advertised. White metal kits are a set of castings and even the best of them requires some preparatory work. Nearly all manufacturers recommend a 'dry run' prior to assembly, that is, to test the fit of everything before final assembly. Do better than that, especially with a complicated model. Spend a few hours just looking at the pieces spread out on the work table. By doing this you will familiarize yourself with all the parts and their location. After that the feel for the model will come naturally and reduce the chances of a silly mistake during construction. Never be afraid to ask or to benefit from the experiences of others. Membership of a model railway club can be a useful way to gain knowledge quickly. Beware of the 'rivet counter', however, he is full of so-called information and criticism and will quote theory at you by the yard. Always about to build a model or a layout, he has an unlimited list of reasons as to why he hasn't actually managed to start anything.

At the beginning of this book it was stated that the aim was to act as a guide to those who would model the LNER be they new or experienced modellers. The subject is vast and a great deal of detailed information on the major operating aspects of the LNER is already in print. Hopefully this book has helped to generate interest in what was, without doubt, one of the finest railways ever to run. If this book has done that then all the hours spent building, painting and lettering, not to mention all the hours spent typing when they should have been spent building, painting and lettering, will have been worth it. Have fun.

Appendices

Appendix A — LNER shed codes

It was LNER practice to indicate on the front buffer beam the shed to which that locomotive was allocated. This was painted on using a two or three letter code, as follows:

Ardsley District
ARD Ardsley
COP Copley Hill (Leeds)

Cambridge District
CAM Cambridge
BSE Bury St Edmunds
KL King's Lynn
SL South Lynn
MAR March
PBE Peterborough East

Colwich District
CLK Colwich
ANN Annesley
LEI Leicester
STV Staveley
WFD Woodford

Darlington District
DAR Darlington
NLN Northallerton
KBY Kirkby Stephen
AUK West Auckland
WHD Wearhead
MIT Middleton Teesdale
LEY Leyburn
MID Middlesbrough
NPT Newport
WHL West Hartlepool
SKN Stockton
HAV Haverton Hill
SAL Saltburn
GUI Guisborough

FYH Ferryhill
EHL East Hartlepool

Doncaster District
DON Doncaster
MEX Mexborough
SHF Sheffield-Darnall
FRO Frodingham
BRN Barnsley

Gateshead District
GHD Gateshead
HTN Heaton Junction
BLA Blaydon
HEX Hexham
ALS Alston
PMN Percy Main
SBH South Blyth
NBH North Blyth
ALN Alnmouth Junction
TWD Tweedmouth
DNS Duns
RMH Reedsmouth
RBY Rothbury

Gorton District
GOR Gorton
TFD Trafford Park
WIG Wigan
LIV Liverpool-Brunswick
WAL Walton on Hill
STP Stockport-Heaton Mersey
NTH Northwich
CHR Chester

WRX   Wrexham
BID   Bidston
Hull District
HLD   Hull-Dairycoates
HLS   Hull-Springhead
HLB   Hull-Botanic Gardens
HLA   Hull-Alexandra Dock
CUD   Cudworth
BRI   Bridlington
King's Cross District
KX   King's Cross
HSY   Hornsey
HAT   Hatfield
HIT   Hitchin
NEA   Neasden
Lincoln District
LIN   Lincoln
IMM   Immingham
LTH   Louth
RET   Retford
TUX   Tuxford
LNG   Langwith
NWH   New Holland
Norwich District
NOR   Norwich
LOW   Lowestoft
YAR   Yarmouth
YB   Yarmouth Beach
MC   Melton Constable
IPS   Ipswich
Peterborough District
NWE   New England
GRA   Grantham
BOS   Boston
Stratford District
STR   Stratford
PKS   Parkeston Quay
COL   Colchester
Sunderland District
SUN   Sunderland
DUR   Durham

BOW   Bowes Bridge
BOR   Borough Gardens
TDK   Tyne Dock
PEL   Pelton Level
CON   Consett Junction
York District
YK   York
SEL   Selby
SCA   Scarborough
WBY   Whitby
MAL   Malton
PKG   Pickering
NMN   Normanton
NEV   Neville Hill
SBK   Starbeck
ILK   Ilkley
PAT   Pately Bridge

Scottish Area
Aberdeen District
ABD   Ferryhill
KIT   Kittybrewster
KEI   Keith
ELG   Elgin
Burntisland District
DEE   Dundee
DFU   Dunfermline Upper
PTH   Perth
STG   Stirling
THJ   Thornton Junction
Edinburgh District
HAY   Haymarket
STM   St Margarets
CAR   Carlisle (Canal)
HAW   Hawick
Glasgow District
EFD   Eastfield
PKD   Parkhead
KPS   Kipps
POL   Polmont
BGT   Bathgate
FW   Fort William

Note

There were, of course, a great many more locomotive sheds than shown here. These were however sub-allocated to one of the depots on this list and were not separately identified on the locomotive. Sub-sheds could be re-allocated from time to time.

Appendix B—Locomotive chassis dimensions

The arrangement of data in this appendix is as follows. Each group of locomotives is identified by wheel arrangement and each class by its letter and number. The first line of figures is the wheel diameter in the order leading, coupled and trailing as appropriate. Each is followed by a figure in brackets indicating the number of spokes in each wheel. The second line of figures gives locomotive wheelbase dimensions between axle centres. All data is tabulated as for a locomotive facing to the left.

4-6-2 Tender

A1   3 ft 2 in (10)   6 ft 8 in (20)   3 ft 8 in (10)
       6 ft 3 in + 5 ft 6 in + 7 ft 3 in + 7 ft 3 in + 9 ft 6 in   (Later Class A10)

A3   3 ft 2 in (10)   6 ft 8 in (20)   3 ft 8 in (10)
       6 ft 3 in + 5 ft 6 in + 7 ft 3 in + 7 ft 3 in + 9 ft 6 in

A4   3 ft 2 in (10)   6 ft 8 in (20)   3 ft 8 in (20)
       6 ft 3 in + 5 ft 6 in + 7 ft 3 in + 7 ft 3 in + 9 ft 6 in

A2   3 ft $1\frac{1}{4}$ in (12)   6 ft 8 in (20)   3 ft $9\frac{1}{4}$ in (10)
       6 ft 6 in + 7 ft 8 in + 7 ft 6 in + 7 ft 6 in + 8 ft 0 in   Raven

A1/1   3 ft 2 in (10)   6 ft 8 in (20)   3 ft 8 in (10)
       6 ft 3 in + 8 ft 2 in + 7 ft 3 in + 7 ft 3 in + 9 ft 6 in   Thompson

A2/1   3 ft 2 in (10)   6 ft 2 in (18)   3 ft 8 in (10)
       6 ft 3 in + 8 ft 2 in + 6 ft 6 in + 6 ft 6 in + 9 ft 3 in   Thompson

A2/2   3 ft 2 in (10)   6 ft 2 in (18)   3 ft 8 in (10)
       6 ft 3 in + 8 ft 2 in + 6 ft 6 in + 6 ft 6 in + 9 ft 6 in   Thompson

A2/3   3 ft 2 in (10)   6 ft 2 in (18)   3 ft 8 in (10)
       6 ft 3 in + 8 ft 2 in + 6 ft 6 in + 6 ft 6 in + 9 ft 6 in   Thompson

A1   3 ft 2 in (10)   6 ft 8 in (20)   3 ft 8 in (10)
       6 ft 3 in + 5 ft 9 in + 7 ft 3 in + 7 ft 3 in + 9 ft 9 in   Peppercorn

A2   3 ft 2 in (10)   6 ft 2 in (18)   3 ft 8 in (10)
       6 ft 3 in + 5 ft 7 in + 6 ft 6 in + 6 ft 6 in + 9 ft 6 in   Peppercorn

4-6-2 Tank

A5   3 ft 6 in (10)   5 ft 7 in (18)   3 ft 9 in (10)
       6 ft 6 in + 7 ft 3 in + 6 ft 6 in + 6 ft 6 in + 6 ft 0 in

A6   3 ft $1\frac{1}{4}$ in (12)   5 ft $1\frac{1}{4}$ in (16)   3 ft $9\frac{1}{4}$ in (10)
       6 ft 6 in + 7 ft 3 in + 6 ft 0 in + 6 ft 6 in + 7 ft 1 in

A7   3 ft $1\frac{1}{4}$ in (12)   4 ft $7\frac{1}{4}$ in (14)   3 ft $9\frac{1}{4}$ in (10)
       6 ft 6 in + 7 ft 3 in + 7 ft 3 in + 7 ft 3 in + 6 ft 0 in

A8   3 ft $1\frac{1}{4}$ in (12)   5 ft 9 in (20)   3 ft 9 in (12)
       6 ft 6 in + 7 ft 3 in + 6 ft 6 in + 6 ft 6 in + 6 ft 6 in

4-6-0 Tender

B1   3 ft 6 in (10)   6 ft 9 in (20)   (Later Class B18)
       6 ft 6 in + 5 ft $9\frac{1}{2}$ in + 7 ft 3 in + 7 ft 3 in

B2   3 ft 6 in (10)   6 ft 9 in (20)   (Later Class B19)
       6 ft 6 in + 6 ft 10 in + 7 ft 3 in + 8 ft 3 in

B3   3 ft 6 in (10)   6 ft 9 in (20)
        6 ft 6 in + 6 ft 10 in + 7 ft 3 in + 8 ft 3 in
B4   3 ft 6 in (10)   6 ft 7 in (20)
        6 ft 6 in + 5 ft $9\frac{1}{2}$ in + 7 ft 3 in + 7 ft 3 in
B5   3 ft 6 in (10)   6 ft 1 in (18)
        6 ft 6 in + 5 ft $7\frac{1}{2}$ in + 7 ft 0 in + 7 ft 0 in
B6   3 ft 6 in (10)   5 ft 8 in (18)
        6 ft 6 in + 5 ft 9 in + 6 ft 9 in + 8 ft 6 in
B7   3 ft 6 in (10)   5 ft 8 in (18)
        6 ft 6 in + 7 ft 4 in + 6 ft 9 in + 7 ft 8 in
B8   3 ft 6 in (10)   5 ft 7 in (18)
        6 ft 6 in + 7 ft 4 in + 6 ft 9 in + 7 ft 8 in
B9   3 ft 6 in (10)   5 ft 4 in (16)
        6 ft 6 in + 5 ft $7\frac{1}{2}$ in + 7 ft 0 in + 7 ft 0 in
B12   3 ft 3 in (10)   6 ft 6 in (20)
        6 ft 6 in + 8 ft 0 in + 7 ft 0 in + 7 ft 0 in
B13   3 ft $7\frac{1}{4}$ in (12)   6 ft $1\frac{1}{4}$ in (18)
        6 ft 6 in + 5 ft $6\frac{1}{2}$ in + 7 ft 0 in + 7 ft 0 in
B14   3 ft $7\frac{1}{4}$ in (12)   6 ft $8\frac{1}{4}$ in (20)
        6 ft 6 in + 5 ft 10 in + 7 ft 7 in + 7 ft 7 in
B15   3 ft $7\frac{1}{4}$ in (12)   6 ft $1\frac{1}{4}$ in (18)
        6 ft 6 in + 5 ft $6\frac{1}{2}$ in + 7 ft 0 in + 7 ft 0 in
B16/1   3 ft 1 in (12)   5 ft 8 in (20)
        6 ft 6 in + 7 ft 8 in + 6 ft 9 in + 6 ft 9 in
B16/2/3 6 ft 6 in + 8 ft 5 in + 6 ft 9 in + 6 ft 9 in
B17   3 ft 2 in (12)   6 ft 8 in (20)
        6 ft 3 in + 5 ft 3 in + 7 ft 3 in + 9 ft 0 in
B1   3 ft 2 in (10)   6 ft 2 in (18)   Thompson
        6 ft 3 in + 5 ft 6 in + 7 ft 3 in + 9 ft 0 in
B2   3 ft 2 in (10)   6 ft 8 in (20)   Thompson rebuild
        6 ft 3 in + 5 ft 8 in + 7 ft 3 in + 9 ft 0 in   Class B17

4-4-2 Tender

C1   3 ft 8 in (10)   6 ft 8 in (20)   3 ft 8 in (10)
        6 ft 3 in + 5 ft 3 in + 6 ft 10 in + 8 ft 0 in
C2   3 ft 8 in (10)   6 ft 8 in (20)   3 ft 8 in (10)
        6 ft 3 in + 5 ft 3 in + 6 ft 10 in + 8 ft 0 in
C4   3 ft 6 in (10)   6 ft 9 in (20)   4 ft 3 in (10)
        6 ft 6 in + 5 ft $9\frac{1}{2}$ in + 7 ft 3 in + 8 ft 3 in
C5   3 ft 6 in (10)   6 ft 9 in (20)   4 ft 3 in (10)
        6 ft 6 in + 5 ft $9\frac{1}{2}$ in + 7 ft 3 in + 8 ft 3 in
C6   3 ft $7\frac{1}{4}$ in (12)   6 ft 10 in (20)   4 ft 0 in (12)
        6 ft 6 in + 5 ft 11 in + 7 ft 7 in + 8 ft 0 in
C7   3 ft $7\frac{1}{4}$ in (12)   6 ft 10 in (20)   4 ft 0 in (12)
        6 ft 6 in + 7 ft 5 in + 7 ft 7 in + 8 ft 0 in

C8   3 ft 7¼ in (12)   7 ft 1¼ in (20)   4 ft 0 in (12)
6 ft 6 in + 7 ft 3 in + 7 ft 6 in + 7 ft 6 in

C9   3 ft 7¼ in (12)   6 ft 10 in (20)   3 ft 8 in (12)
6 ft 7 in + 7 ft 5 in + 7 ft 7 in + 8 ft 7½ in + 8 ft 9 in + 10 ft 1½ in + 6 ft 6 in *

*Booster fitted loco with articulated bogie tender

C10   3 ft 6 in (10)   6 ft 9 in (21)   4 ft 3 in (12)
6 ft 6 in + 5 ft 9½ in + 7 ft 3 in + 8 ft 3 in

C11   3 ft 6 in (10)   6 ft 9 in (21)   4 ft 3 in (12)
6 ft 6 in + 5 ft 9½ in + 7 ft 3 in + 8 ft 3 in

4-4-2 Tank

C12   3 ft 8 in (10)   5 ft 8 in (18)   3 ft 8 in (10)
6 ft 3 in + 6 ft 9 in + 8 ft 3 in + 6 ft 0 in

C13   3 ft 6 in (10)   5 ft 7 in (18)   3 ft 9 in (11)
6 ft 0 in + 7 ft 5 in + 9 ft 1 in + 7 ft 4½ in

C14   3 ft 6 in (10)   5 ft 7 in (18)   3 ft 9 in (11)
6 ft 0 in + 7 ft 5 in + 9 ft 1 in + 7 ft 4½ in

C15   3 ft 6 in (10)   5 ft 9 in (18)   3 ft 9 in (10)
6 ft 6 in + 6 ft 7 in + 8 ft 3 in + 7 ft 6 in

C16   3 ft 6 in (10)   5 ft 9 in (18)   3 ft 9 in (10)
6 ft 6 in + 6 ft 8½ in + 8 ft 3 in + 7 ft 6 in

C17   3 ft 0 in (9)   6 ft 0 in (18)   3 ft 7 in (12)
6 ft 6 in + 7 ft 0 in + 8 ft 6 in + 7 ft 6 in

4-4-0 Tender

D1   3 ft 8 in (10)   6 ft 8 in (20)
6 ft 5½ in + 6 ft 8 in + 9 ft 0 in

D2   3 ft 8 in (10)   6 ft 8 in (20)
6 ft 3 in + 6 ft 9 in + 9 ft 0 in

D3   3 ft 8 in (10)   6 ft 8 in (20)
6 ft 3 in + 6 ft 9 in + 8 ft 3 in

D4   3 ft 8 in (10)   6 ft 8 in (20)
6 ft 3 in + 6 ft 9 in + 8 ft 3 in

D5   3 ft 6 in (10)   7 ft 0 in (20)
5 ft 9 in + 7 ft 5 in + 9 ft 0 in

D6   3 ft 6 in (10)   7 ft 0 in (20)
5 ft 9 in + 7 ft 5 in + 9 ft 0 in

D7   3 ft 6 in (10)   6 ft 9 in (20)
5 ft 9 in + 7 ft 5 in + 8 ft 7 in

D8   3 ft 6½ in (10)   6 ft 9½ in (18)
6 ft 0 in + 7 ft 6 in + 8 ft 6 in

D9   3 ft 6 in (10)   6 ft 9 in (20)
6 ft 0 in + 8 ft 1¾ in + 9 ft 9 in

D10   3 ft 6 in (10)   6 ft 9 in (20)
6 ft 6 in + 8 ft 9 in + 10 ft 0 in

D11   3 ft 6 in (10)   6 ft 9 in (20)
6 ft 6 in + 8 ft 9 in + 10 ft 0 in

D12   3 ft 3½ in (10)   6 ft 3½ in (18)
6 ft 0 in + 6 ft 9½ in + 8 ft 0 in

D13   3 ft 1 in (8)   7 ft 0 in (20)
6 ft 3 in + 6 ft 4½ in + 8 ft 9 in

D14   3 ft 9 in (10)   7 ft 0 in (20)
6 ft 6 in + 8 ft 0 in + 9 ft 0 in

D15   3 ft 9 in (10)   7 ft 0 in (20)
6 ft 6 in + 8 ft 0 in + 9 ft 0 in

D16   3 ft 9 in (10)   7 ft 0 in (20)
6 ft 6 in + 8 ft 0 in + 9 ft 0 in

D17   3 ft 7¼ in (12)   7 ft 1¼ in (20)
6 ft 6 in + 7 ft 9 in + 9 ft 3 in

D18   3 ft 7¼ in (12)   7 ft 7¼ in (20)
6 ft 6 in + 7 ft 9 in + 9 ft 6 in

D19   3 ft 7¼ in (12)   7 ft 1¼ in (20)
6 ft 6 in + 7 ft 9 in + 9 ft 3 in

D20   4 ft 0 in (12)   6 ft 10 in (20)
6 ft 6 in + 7 ft 9 in + 9 ft 6 in

D21 3 ft $7\frac{1}{4}$ in (12) 6 ft 10 in (20)
   6 ft 6 in $+ 7$ ft 9 in $+ 9$ ft 6 in
D22 3 ft $7\frac{1}{4}$ in (12) 6 ft 8 in (20)
   6 ft 6 in $+ 6$ ft 9 in $+ 8$ ft 8 in
D23 3 ft $1\frac{1}{4}$ in (12) 6 ft $1\frac{1}{4}$ in (18)
   6 ft 6 in $+ 6$ ft 7 in $+ 8$ ft $1\frac{1}{2}$ in
D24 3 ft 9 in (11) 6 ft 6 in (20)
   6 ft 6 in $+ 7$ ft 3 in $+ 9$ ft 3 in
D25 3 ft 6 in (10) 7 ft 0 in (22)
   6 ft 6 in $+ 6$ ft 7 in $+ 9$ ft 3 in
D26 3 ft 6 in (10) 6 ft 6 in (22)
   6 ft 6 in $+ 7$ ft 7 in $+ 9$ ft 6 in
D27 3 ft 6 in (10) 6 ft 6 in (22)
   6 ft 6 in $+ 6$ ft 7 in $+ 9$ ft 0 in
D28 3 ft 6 in (10) 6 ft 6 in (22)
   6 ft 6 in $+ 6$ ft 7 in $+ 9$ ft 0 in
D29 3 ft 6 in (10) 6 ft 6 in (22)
   6 ft 6 in $+ 7$ ft 7 in $+ 9$ ft 6 in
D30 3 ft 6 in (10) 6 ft 6 in (22)
   6 ft 6 in $+ 7$ ft 7 in $+ 9$ ft 6 in
D31 3 ft 6 in (10) 6 ft 6 in (22)
   6 ft 6 in $+ 6$ ft 7 in $+ 9$ ft 0 in
D32 3 ft 6 in (10) 6 ft 0 in (20)
   6 ft 6 in $+ 7$ ft 7 in $+ 9$ ft 6 in
D33 3 ft 6 in (10) 6 ft 0 in (20)
   6 ft 6 in $+ 7$ ft 7 in $+ 9$ ft 6 in
D34 3 ft 6 in (10) 6 ft 0 in (20)
   6 ft 6 in $+ 7$ ft 7 in $+ 9$ ft 6 in
D35 3 ft 6 in (10) 5 ft 7 in (16)
   6 ft 6 in $+ 6$ ft 7 in $+ 8$ ft 2 in
D36 3 ft 6 in (10) 5 ft 7 in (16)

   6 ft 6 in $+ 6$ ft 7 in $+ 9$ ft 1 in
D38 3 ft $9\frac{1}{2}$ in (11) 6 ft $6\frac{1}{2}$ in (20)
   5 ft 6 in $+ 7$ ft 5 in $+ 8$ ft 9 in
D39 3 ft $0\frac{1}{2}$ in (10) 6 ft 1 in (20)
   6 ft 0 in $+ 6$ ft 6 in $+ 8$ ft 0 in
D40 3 ft $9\frac{1}{2}$ in (11) 6 ft 1 in (20)
   5 ft 6 in $+ 7$ ft $6\frac{1}{2}$ in $+ 8$ ft 9 in
D41 3 ft $9\frac{1}{2}$ in (11) 6 ft 1 in (20)
   5 ft 6 in $+ 7$ ft $6\frac{1}{2}$ in $+ 8$ ft 9 in
D42 3 ft $9\frac{1}{2}$ in (11) 6 ft $0\frac{1}{2}$ in (20)
   5 ft 6 in $+ 7$ ft 5 in $+ 8$ ft 9 in
D43 3 ft $9\frac{1}{2}$ in (11) 6 ft $0\frac{1}{2}$ in (20)
   5 ft 6 in $+ 7$ ft 5 in $+ 8$ ft 9 in
D44 3 ft 0 in (9) 6 ft 0 in (18)
   5 ft 6 in $+ 7$ ft 2 in $+ 8$ ft 0 in
D45 3 ft $0\frac{1}{2}$ in (10) 5 ft 7 in (18)
   6 ft 0 in $+ 6$ ft $6\frac{1}{2}$ in $+ 8$ ft 0 in
D46 3 ft 1 in (9) 5 ft 7 in (18)
   5 ft 6 in $+ 7$ ft $4\frac{1}{2}$ in $+ 8$ ft 4 in
D47 3 ft 0 in (10) 5 ft $6\frac{1}{2}$ in (18)
   6 ft 0 in $+ 6$ ft 6 in $+ 8$ ft 0 in
D48 3 ft 0 in (9) 5 ft 6 in (18)
   5 ft 6 in $+ 7$ ft 2 in $+ 8$ ft 0 in
D49 3 ft $1\frac{1}{4}$ in (12) 6 ft 8 in (20)
   6 ft 6 in $+ 8$ ft 5 in $+ 10$ ft 0 in
D52 3 ft $3\frac{1}{2}$ in (10) 6 ft $6\frac{1}{2}$ in (20)
   6 ft 0 in $+ 7$ ft $0\frac{1}{2}$ in $+ 8$ ft 6 in
D53 3 ft $3\frac{1}{2}$ in (10) 6 ft $6\frac{1}{2}$ in (20)
   6 ft 0 in $+ 7$ ft $0\frac{1}{2}$ in $+ 8$ ft 6 in
D54 3 ft $3\frac{1}{2}$ in (10) 6 ft $6\frac{1}{2}$ in (20)
   6 ft 0 in $+ 7$ ft $0\frac{1}{2}$ in $+ 8$ ft 6 in

4-4-0 Tank

D50 3 ft 6 in (10) 6 ft 0 in (20)   D51 2 ft 6 in (Disc) 5 ft 0 in (16)
   6 ft 6 in $+ 6$ ft 7 in $+ 8$ ft 0 in 5 ft 0 in $+ 5$ ft $10\frac{1}{2}$ in $+ 7$ ft 0 in

2-4-0 Tender

E1 4 ft 2 in (13) 6 ft 8 in (20)
   9 ft 8 in $+ 8$ ft 3 in
E2 4 ft $3\frac{1}{2}$ in (13) 6 ft $9\frac{1}{2}$ in (20)
   7 ft 11 in $+ 8$ ft 6 in
E4 4 ft 0 in (12) 5 ft 8 in (16)
   7 ft 9 in $+ 8$ ft 9 in
E5 4 ft 6 in (16) 7 ft 0 in (20)
   8 ft 0 in $+ 8$ ft 8 in
E7 4 ft $2\frac{1}{2}$ in (12) 6 ft 1 in (20)
   7 ft 3 in $+ 7$ ft 9 in

2-4-0 Tank

E8 3 ft $9\frac{1}{2}$ in (not known) 5 ft $6\frac{1}{2}$ in (not known)
   7 ft 3 in $+ 7$ ft 9 in

2-4-2 Tank

F1	3 ft 6 in (10)	5 ft 7 in (18)	3 ft 6 in (10)
	7 ft 10½ in + 8 ft 7 in + 7 ft 0 in		
F2	3 ft 6 in (10)	5 ft 7 in (18)	3 ft 6 in (10)
	7 ft 10½ in + 8 ft 7 in + 7 ft 0 in		
F3	4 ft 0 in (10)	5 ft 8 in (16)	4 ft 0 in (10)
	7 ft 6 in + 8 ft 9 in + 7 ft 0 in		
F4	3 ft 9 in (10)	5 ft 4 in (16)	3 ft 9 in (10)
	7 ft 6 in + 8 ft 0 in + 7 ft 6 in		
F5	3 ft 9 in (10)	5 ft 4 in (16)	3 ft 9 in (10)
	7 ft 6 in + 8 ft 0 in + 7 ft 6 in		
F6	3 ft 9 in (10)	5 ft 4 in (16)	3 ft 9 in (10)
	7 ft 6 in + 8 ft 0 in + 7 ft 6 in		
F7	3 ft 6 in (10)	4 ft 10 in (16)	3 ft 6 in (10)
	6 ft 3 in + 7 ft 0 in + 6 ft 3 in		
F8	3 ft 9¼ in (10)	5 ft 7¼ in (16)	3 ft 9¼ in (10)
	7 ft 6 in + 8 ft 1½ in + 7 ft 6 in		
F9	3 ft 2 in (9)	5 ft 1 in (16)	3 ft 2 in (9)
	6 ft 9 in + 7 ft 0 in + 6 ft 8 in		

0-4-4 Tank

G1	5 ft 8 in (18)	3 ft 2 in (10)	G6	5 ft 6 in (16)		3 ft 4 in (10)
	7 ft 3 in + 10 ft 3 in + 5 ft 0 in			7 ft 8 in + 9 ft 0 in + 5 ft 0 in		
G2	5 ft 2 in (16)	3 ft 2 in (10)	G7	5 ft 9 in (18)		3 ft 6 in (10)
	7 ft 3 in + 10 ft 3 in + 5 ft 0 in			7 ft 6 in + 8 ft 3 in + 6 ft 6 in		
G3	5 ft 6 in (15)	3 ft 0 in (9)	G8	5 ft 9 in (18)		3 ft 6 in (10)
	7 ft 9 in + 9 ft 0 in + 5 ft 6 in			7 ft 6 in + 8 ft 0 in + 6 ft 6 in		
G4	4 ft 11 in (15)	3 ft 1 in (8)	G9	5 ft 9 in (18)		3 ft 6 in (10)
	7 ft 7 in + 9 ft 9 in + 5 ft 0 in			7 ft 6 in + 8 ft 3 in + 6 ft 6 in		
G5	5 ft 1¼ in (16)	3 ft 1¼ in (12)	G10	5 ft 0 in (16)		3 ft 0½ in (9)
	7 ft 9 in + 9 ft 0 in + 5 ft 9 in			7 ft 6 in + 9 ft 0 in + 5 ft 6 in		

4-4-4 Tank

H1	3 ft 1¼ in (12)	5 ft 9 in (18)	3 ft 1¼ in (12)
	6 ft 6 in + 7 ft 3 in + 8 ft 0 in + 6 ft 3 in + 6 ft 6 in		
H2	3 ft 0 in (9)	5 ft 9 in (18)	3 ft 0 in (9)
	6 ft 6 in + 7 ft 4½ in + 7 ft 9 in + 5 ft 4½ in + 6 ft 6 in		

0-6-0 Tender

J1	5 ft 8 in (18)	J4	5 ft 2 in (16)
	7 ft 3 in + 9 ft 0 in		7 ft 3 in + 8 ft 3 in
J2	5 ft 8 in (18)	J5	5 ft 2 in (16)
	7 ft 3 in + 9 ft 0 in		7 ft 3 in + 9 ft 0 in
J3	5 ft 2 in (16)	J6	5 ft 2 in (16)
	7 ft 3 in + 8 ft 3 in		7 ft 3 in + 9 ft 0 in

J7	4 ft 8 in (14)		7 ft 3 in + 8 ft 3 in
	7 ft 3 in + 8 ft 3 in	J24	4 ft 7¼ in (14)
J8	5 ft 4 in (16)		7 ft 9 in + 8 ft 0 in
	7 ft 5 in + 7 ft 9 in	J25	4 ft 7¼ in (14)
J9	5 ft 1 in (13)		8 ft 0 in + 8 ft 6 in
	7 ft 11 in + 8 ft 7 in	J26	4 ft 7¼ in (14)
J10	5 ft 1 in (13)		8 ft 0 in + 8 ft 6 in
	7 ft 11 in + 8 ft 7 in	J27	4 ft 7¼ in (14)
J11	5 ft 2 in (13)		8 ft 0 in + 8 ft 6 in
	8 ft 1 in + 9 ft 0 in	J28	5 ft 0 in (16)
J12	4 ft 9½ in (16)		7 ft 9 in + 9 ft 3 in
	7 ft 7 in + 7 ft 7 in	J31	5 ft 1¾ in (12/16)
J13	4 ft 10 in (16)		7 ft 3 in + 7 ft 9 in
	7 ft 11 in + 8 ft 7 in	J32	5 ft 0 in (16)
J14	4 ft 11 in (13)		7 ft 6 in + 8 ft 0 in
	7 ft 7 in + 8 ft 6 in	J33	5 ft 0 in (16)
J15	4 ft 11 in (13)		7 ft 6 in + 8 ft 0 in
	7 ft 7 in + 8 ft 6 in	J34	5 ft 0 in (16)
J16	4 ft 11 in (13)		7 ft 6 in + 9 ft 0 in
	8 ft 10 in + 8 ft 10 in	J35	5 ft 0 in (16)
J17	4 ft 11 in (13)		7 ft 9 in + 9 ft 0 in
	8 ft 10 in + 8 ft 10 in	J36	5 ft 0 in (16)
J18	4 ft 11 in (13)		7 ft 6 in + 8 ft 0 in
	8 ft 10 in + 8 ft 10 in	J37	5 ft 0 in (16)
J19	4 ft 11 in (13)		7 ft 9 in + 9 ft 2 in
	8 ft 10 in + 8 ft 10 in	J38	4 ft 8 in (14)
J20	4 ft 11 in (13)		8 ft 0 in + 9 ft 0 in
	8 ft 10 in + 10 ft 0 in	J39	5 ft 2 in (16)
J21	5 ft 1¼ in (16)		8 ft 0 in + 9 ft 0 in
	8 ft 0 in + 8 ft 6 in	J40	5 ft 3 in (16)
J22	5 ft 1 in/5 ft 7¼ in (16)		8 ft 0 in + 8 ft 6 in
	7 ft 9 in + 8 ft 3 in	J41	5 ft 3 in (16)
J23	5 ft 0 in (16)		8 ft 0 in + 8 ft 6 in

0-6-0 Tank

J50	4 ft 8 in (14)	J55	4 ft 8 in (14)
	7 ft 3 in + 9 ft 0 in		7 ft 3 in + 8 ft 3 in
J51	4 ft 8 in (14)	J56	4 ft 8 in (14)
	7 ft 3 in + 9 ft 0 in		7 ft 3 in + 7 ft 7 in
J52	4 ft 8 in (14)	J57	4 ft 0½ in (12)
	7 ft 3 in + 8 ft 3 in		7 ft 3 in + 8 ft 3 in
J53	4 ft 8 in (14)	J58	5 ft 1¼ in (16)
	7 ft 3 in + 8 ft 3 in		7 ft 5 in + 7 ft 9 in
J54	4 ft 8 in (14)	J59	4 ft 9½ in (15)
	7 ft 3 in + 8 ft 3 in		7 ft 0 in + 7 ft 4 in

J60 4 ft 7 in (13)
7 ft 0 in + 7 ft 0 in

J61 3 ft 9 in (12)/3 ft 1½ in (10)
6 ft 3 in + 6 ft 6 in/5 ft 6 in
+ 5 ft 0 in

J62 3 ft 6 in (10)
6 ft 0 in + 6 ft 0 in

J63 3 ft 6 in (10)
6 ft 0 in + 6 ft 0 in

J64 3 ft 4½ in (10)
6 ft 0 in + 6 ft 0 in/5 ft 9 in
+ 5 ft 9 in

J65 4 ft 0 in (10)
6 ft 4 in + 7 ft 0 in

J66 4 ft 0 in (10/16)
6 ft 4 in + 7 ft 0 in

J67 4 ft 0 in (10/16)
6 ft 4 in + 7 ft 6 in

J68 4 ft 0 in (10/12/16)
6 ft 4 in + 7 ft 6 in

J69 4 ft 0 in (10/15)
6 ft 4 in + 7 ft 6 in

J70 3 ft 1 in (10)
3 ft 4 in + 3 ft 4 in

J71 4 ft 7¼ in (12/14)
6 ft 6 in + 7 ft 2 in

J72 4 ft 1¼ in (12)
6 ft 8 in + 7 ft 0 in

J73 4 ft 7¼ in (14)
7 ft 6 in + 8 ft 2 in

J74 4 ft 7¼ in (14)
7 ft 9 in + 8 ft 0 in

J75 4 ft 6 in (16)

7 ft 3 in + 8 ft 3 in

J76 4 ft 9 in (14)
7 ft 8 in + 8 ft 0 in

J77 4 ft 1¼ in (12)
7 ft 8 in + 8 ft 6 in

J78 3 ft 6¼ in (9/10)
6 ft 0 in + 4 ft 0 in

J79 3 ft 6¼ in (10)
6 ft 0 in + 5 ft 0 in

J80 5 ft 0 in (16)
7 ft 3 in + 8 ft 3 in

J81 5 ft 0 in (16)
7 ft 0 in + 7 ft 3 in

J82 4 ft 6 in (14)
6 ft 4 in + 6 ft 10 in

J83 4 ft 6 in (14)
7 ft 6 in + 8 ft 0 in

J84 4 ft 3 in (14)
6 ft 6 in + 8 ft 0 in

J85 4 ft 3 in (12)
7 ft 0 in + 7 ft 0 in

J86 5 ft 0 in (16)
7 ft 3 in + 7 ft 9 in

J88 4 ft 8¼ in (10)
5 ft 3 in + 5 ft 9 in

J90 4 ft 6 in (13)
6 ft 10 in + 6 ft 10 in

J91 4 ft 6 in (12)
6 ft 10 in + 6 ft 10 in

J93 3 ft 7 in (10/12)
6 ft 3 in + 7 ft 6 in

J94 4 ft 3 in (14)
5 ft 9 in + 5 ft 3 in

2-6-0 Tender

K1 3 ft 2 in (10)   5 ft 8 in (18)
8 ft 7 in + 7 ft 3 in + 9 ft 0 in

K2 3 ft 2 in (10)   5 ft 8 in (18)
8 ft 11 in + 7 ft 3 in + 9 ft 0 in

K3 3 ft 2 in (10)   5 ft 8 in (18)
8 ft 11 in + 7 ft 6 in + 8 ft 9 in

K4 3 ft 2 in (10)   5 ft 2 in (16)
8 ft 11 in + 7 ft 6 in + 8 ft 9 in

K5 3 ft 2 in (10)   5 ft 8 in (18)   Thompson rebuild,
8 ft 11 in + 7 ft 6 in + 8 ft 9 in   one loco only

K1   3 ft 2 in (10)   5 ft 2 in (16)
        8 ft 11 in + 7 ft 6 in + 8 ft 9 in   Thompson/Peppercorn

2-6-4 Tank

L1   3 ft 0 in (9)   5 ft 1 in (16)   3 ft 9 in (9)
        6 ft 3 in + 8 ft 8 in + 8 ft 4 in + 6 ft 9 in + 7 ft 6 in   Later Class
                                                                    L3
L2   3 ft 1 in (10)   5 ft 6 in (18)   3 ft 1 in (10)
        8 ft 10 in + 7 ft 3 in + 8 ft 3 in + 6 ft 3 in + 6 ft 0 in
L1   3 ft 2 in (10)   5 ft 2 in (16)   3 ft 2 in (10)
        8 ft 7 in + 6 ft 6 in + 7 ft 0 in + 6 ft 2 in + 6 ft 3 in   Thompson

0-6-4 Tank

M1   4 ft 9 in (13)   3 ft 0 in (9)
        7 ft 10 in + 8 ft 8 in + 5 ft 6 in + 7 ft 6 in
M2   5 ft 9 in (18)   3 ft 6 in (10)
        7 ft 9 in + 8 ft 3 in + 6 ft 3 in + 6 ft 6 in

0-6-2 Tank

N1   5 ft 8 in (18)   3 ft 8 in (10)
        7 ft 3 in + 9 ft 0 in + 7 ft 0 in (7 ft 6 in) — on some parts of class
N2   5 ft 8 in (18)   3 ft 8 in (10)
        7 ft 3 in + 9 ft 0 in + 7 ft 6 in
N4   5 ft 1 in (13)   3 ft 6 in (10)
        7 ft 11 in + 8 ft 7 in + 6 ft 0 in
N5   5 ft 1 in (13)   3 ft 6 in (10)
        7 ft 11 in + 8 ft 7 in + 6 ft 0 in
N6   4 ft 9 in (13)   3 ft 9 in (10)
        7 ft 10 in + 7 ft 2 in + 7 ft 6 in
N7   4 ft 10 in (13)   3 ft 9 in/3 ft 6 in (10)
        7 ft 6 in + 8 ft 9 in + 6 ft 9 in
N8   5 ft 1$\frac{1}{4}$ in (16)   3 ft 9$\frac{1}{4}$ in (10)
        8 ft 0 in + 8 ft 6 in + 6 ft 0 in
N9   5 ft 1$\frac{1}{4}$ in (16)   3 ft 9$\frac{1}{4}$ in (10)
        8 ft 0 in + 8 ft 6 in + 6 ft 0 in
N10   4 ft 7$\frac{1}{4}$ in (14)   3 ft 9$\frac{1}{4}$ in (10)
        8 ft 0 in + 8 ft 6 in + 6 ft 0 in
N11   4 ft 9 in (13)   3 ft 9 in (10)
        7 ft 10 in + 7 ft 2 in + 7 ft 6 in
N12   4 ft 6 in (16)   3 ft 9 in (11)
        7 ft 3 in + 8 ft 3 in + 7 ft 6 in
N13   4 ft 6 in (14)   3 ft 9 in (11)
        7 ft 3 in + 8 ft 3 in + 7 ft 6 in
N14   4 ft 6 in (14)   3 ft 9 in (10)
        7 ft 6 in + 8 ft 0 in + 7 ft 0 in
N15   4 ft 6 in (14)   3 ft 9 in (10)
        7 ft 6 in + 8 ft 0 in + 7 ft 0 in

N18   4 ft 6 in (12)   3 ft 8 in (10)
           7 ft 0 in + 7 ft 0 in + 6 ft 0 in
N19   3 ft 9 in (12)   3 ft 0 in (10)
           5 ft 0 in + 4 ft 6 in + 8 ft 0 in

2-8-0 Tender

01   3 ft 2 in (10)   4 ft 8 in (14)
        7 ft 10 in + 6 ft 0 in + 6 ft 6 in + 6 ft 0 in   Later Class 03
02   2 ft 8 in (10)   4 ft 8 in (14)
        8 ft 8 in + 6 ft 6 in + 6 ft 0 in + 6 ft 0 in
04   3 ft 6 in (10)   4 ft 8 in (14)
        8 ft 4 in + 5 ft $8\frac{1}{2}$ in + 5 ft $5\frac{1}{2}$ in + 5 ft 11 in
05   3 ft 6 in (10)   4 ft 8 in (14)
        8 ft 4 in + 5 ft $8\frac{1}{2}$ in + 5 ft $5\frac{1}{2}$ in + 5 ft 11 in
01   3 ft 6 in (10)   4 ft 8 in (14)
        8 ft 4 in + 5 ft $8\frac{1}{2}$ in + 5 ft $5\frac{1}{2}$ in + 5 ft 11 in Thompson rebuild of
                                                            Class 04
06   3 ft $3\frac{1}{2}$ in (10)   4 ft $8\frac{1}{2}$ in (15)
        8 ft 9 in + 5 ft 6 in + 5 ft 6 in + 6 ft 3 in
07   3 ft 2 in (disc)   4 ft $8\frac{1}{2}$ in (12)
        8 ft 7 in + 5 ft 3 in + 5 ft 3 in + 5 ft 9 in

2-8-2 Tender

P1   3 ft 2 in (10)   5 ft 2 in (16)   3 ft 8 in (10)
        8 ft 8 in + 6 ft 6 in + 6 ft 0 in + 6 ft 0 in + 9 ft 0 in
P2   3 ft 2 in (10)   6 ft 2 in (18)   3 ft 8 in (10)

0-8-0 Tender

Q1   4 ft 8 in (14)
        6 ft 0 in + 5 ft 8 in + 6 ft 0 in
Q2   4 ft 8 in (14)
        6 ft 0 in + 5 ft 8 in + 6 ft 0 in
Q3   4 ft 8 in (14)
        6 ft 0 in + 5 ft 8 in + 6 ft 0 in
Q4   4 ft 8 in (14)
        5 ft $8\frac{1}{2}$ in + 5 ft $5\frac{1}{2}$ in + 5 ft 11 in
Q5   4 ft $7\frac{1}{4}$ in (14)
        5 ft 7 in + 5 ft 7 in + 6 ft 0 in
Q6   4 ft $7\frac{1}{4}$ in (14)
        5 ft 7 in + 5 ft 7 in + 6 ft 0 in
Q7   4 ft $7\frac{1}{4}$ in (14)
        7 ft 0 in + 5 ft 9 in + 5 ft 9 in
Q10   4 ft 6 in (13)
        6 ft 0 in + 5 ft 3 in + 5 ft 3 in

0-8-0 Tank
Q1   4 ft 8 in (14)   Thompson rebuild of Class Q4 tender locos
     5 ft 8½ in + 5 ft 5½ in + 5 ft 11 in

0-8-2 Tank
R1   4 ft 8 in (14)   3 ft 8 in (10)
     6 ft 0 in + 5 ft 8 in + 6 ft 0 in + 7 ft 6 in

0-8-4 Tank
S1   4 ft 8 in (14)   3 ft 6 in (10)
     5 ft 8½ in + 5 ft 5½ in + 5 ft 11 in + 6 ft 1 in + 7 ft
     6 in   Saturated
     4 ft 8 in (14)   3 ft 2 in (10)
5 ft 8½ in + 5 ft 5½ in + 5 ft 11 in + 5 ft 7 in + 8 ft 6 in   Superheated

4-8-0 Tank
     3 ft 1¼ in (12)   4 ft 7¼ in (14)
     6 ft 6 in + 7 ft 3 in + 5 ft 1 in + 5 ft 1 in + 5 ft 1 in

2-8-0 + 0-8-2
     2 ft 8 in (disc)   4 ft 8 in (14)
     8 ft 8 in + 6 ft 6 in + 5 ft 8¼ in + 5 ft 8¼ in   Reversed for second
                                                        unit

2-6-2 Tank
V1/V3   3 ft 2 in (10)   5 ft 8 in (18)   3 ft 8 in (10)
        8 ft 6 in + 7 ft 3 in + 9 ft 0 in + 7 ft 6 in

2-6-2 Tender
V2   3 ft 2 in (10)   6 ft 2 in (18)   3 ft 8 in (10)
     8 ft 11 in + 7 ft 3 in + 8 ft 3 in + 9 ft 3 in
V4   3 ft 2 in (10)   5 ft 8 in (18)   3 ft 2 in (10)
     8 ft 6 in + 6 ft 6 in + 6 ft 4 in + 8 ft 0 in

4-6-4 Tender
W1   3 ft 2 in (10)   6 ft 8 in (20)   3 ft 2 in (10)
     6 ft 6 in + 5 ft 6 in + 7 ft 3 in + 7 ft 3 in + 7 ft 6 in + 6 ft 0 in

2-2-4 Tank
X1   3 ft 7 in (10)   5 ft 7¾ in (16)   3 ft 1¼ in (10)
     7 ft 8 in + 7 ft 8 in + 5 ft 3 in
X2   4 ft 1¼ in (10)   6 ft 1¼ in (18)   3 ft 0 in (10)
     8 ft 4 in + 9 ft 0 in + 5 ft 0 in
X3   4 ft 0 in (10)   6 ft 6½ in (20)   3 ft 1¼ in (10)
     8 ft 10 in + 8 ft 1½ in + 5 ft 3 in

4-2-2 Tender
X4   3 ft 6 in (10)   7 ft 9 in (22)   4 ft 6 in (12)
       5 ft 9 in + 7 ft 5 in + 9 ft 9 in

0-4-0 Tank

Y1	2 ft 6 in (disc)	Y6	3 ft 1 in (8)
	7 ft 0 in		6 ft 6 in
Y2	3 ft 0 in (10)	Y7	3 ft 6¼ in (10)
	5 ft 6 in		6 ft 0 in
Y3	2 ft 6 in (disc)	Y8	3 ft 0 in (9)
	7 ft 0 in		6 ft 0 in
Y4	3 ft 10 in (10)	Y9	3 ft 8 in (10)
	6 ft 0 in		7 ft 0 in
Y5	3 ft 7 in (10)	Y10	3 ft 2 in (10)
	5 ft 9 in		6 ft 0 in

0-4-0 Tender
Y10   4 ft 3 in (10)
        7 ft 6 in

0-4-2 Tank
Z4   3 ft 6 in (11)   2 ft 9 in (8)
Z5   4 ft 0 in (12)   2 ft 9 in (8)

Note
Where more than one figure is shown in any column this indicates that there were minor variations within the class. This may apply to a single locomotive and may also have been applied for a limited period following a works visit.

Appendix C — Coach dimensions

Type	Length of set	Bogie centres	Length of frame	Length of body	Height (rail)	Width (max)
Gresley mainline stock	—	43 ft	60 ft	61 ft 6 in	12 ft 10 in	9 ft or 9 ft 3 in
Locker composite	—	47 ft	65 ft	66 ft 6 in	12 ft 10 in	9 ft 3 in
Cambridge stock	—	35 ft	51 ft	52 ft 6 in	12 ft 10 in	9 ft 3 in
1935 Artic steel twins	105 ft 1 in	43 ft 3$\frac{1}{2}$ in	52 ft	52 ft 9 in	12 ft 10 in	9 ft 3 in
1935 steel stock	—	35 ft	51 ft	52 ft 6 in	12 ft 10 in	9 ft 3 in
Tourist artic stock	107 ft 1 in	43 ft 3$\frac{1}{2}$ in	51 ft 2$\frac{1}{4}$ in	51 ft 11$\frac{1}{4}$ in	12 ft 10 in	9 ft 3 in
Tourist, buffet and open third	—	43 ft	60 ft	61 ft 6 in	12 ft 10 in	9 ft 3 in
1924 Triplet restaurant Outer cars	153 ft 7 in	47 ft	54 ft 5$\frac{1}{2}$ in	55 ft 2$\frac{1}{2}$ in		
Centre car		42 ft 1 in	41 ft	41 ft	12 ft 10 in	9 ft 3 in
1926 First artic twin sleepers	113 ft 6 in	47 ft	55 ft 5$\frac{1}{2}$ in	56 ft 2$\frac{1}{2}$ in	12 ft 10 in	9 ft 3 in

Vehicle						
Gresley non-corridor stock	—	35 ft	51 ft 1½ in	51 ft 1½ in	12 ft 10 in	9 ft or 9 ft 3 in
Gresley non-corridor artic twins	103 ft 3½ in	42 ft 7¼ in	51 ft 1½ in	51 ft 1½ in	12 ft 10 in	9 ft or 9 ft 3 in
1933 TPO vans	—	43 ft	60 ft	60 ft 1½ in	12 ft 10 in	9 ft 3 in
Gresley non-corridor artic twin Dia210/313	115 ft 8 in	47 ft	55 ft 4¾ in	55 ft 6¼ in	12 ft 10 in	9 ft 3 in
Thompson corridor stock (except composite)		43 ft 6 in	61 ft 6 in	63 ft	12 ft 10 in	9 ft 3 in
Composite	—	40 ft	58 ft	59 ft 6 in	12 ft 10 in	9 ft 3 in
Matchboard full brake	—	43 ft 6 in	61 ft 6 in	63 ft	12 ft 10 in	8 ft 9 in
Thompson non-corridor stock		36 ft	52 ft 4 in	52 ft 2½ in	12 ft 10 in	9 ft 3 in
Gresley Quad-art	166 ft 2½ in OR	39 ft 3 in / 35 ft 9 in	38 ft 1¼ in / 43 ft 6 in	38 ft 1¼ in / 43 ft 6 in	12 ft 10 in / 12 ft 10 in	9 ft / 9 ft

Note

These sets ran in two pairs of Quad-arts making eight vehicles in all. They were arranged as follows: short third, brake/short third/long third/long third, first composite/long first, third composite/short all second/short second, brake.

Appendix D — Chronology

1923 Amalgamation of GNR, NER, NBR, GNoSR, GCR and GER to form The London & North Eastern Railway.

31 January Inspection of proposed locomotive liveries at York.

22 February Inspection of proposed locomotive liveries at Marylebone.

23 February Inspection of coaching stock liveries at Marylebone.

March Adoption of standard livery and lettering styles for locomotives.

September Ampersand dropped from company initials on locomotives. Suffix scheme introduced for numbering of absorbed locomotives. Suffix scheme adopted for coaching stock to show line of origin of absorbed stock.
Revised locomotive classification scheme approved.
RCH pattern cast iron split axleboxes adopted for new freight stock.
All fitted freight vans and wagons to be painted brown red oxide.

1924 Revised numbering scheme introduced for locomotives with first digit indicating line of origin.

1925 Coach numbering revised, suffix letter discontinued and prefix number added to show line of origin and operation
Sentinel-Cammell steam railcars introduced.
Ends of non-corridor stock now painted black.

1926 Non-common user vehicles identified by 'N' on ends.

1927 Clayton steam railcars introduced.

1928 Position of LNER on coaching stock moved from body centre to panel LHS with number to RHS.

November Tender locos number moved from tender to cab side.
Toad D introduced.

1929 LNER designed TPO vehicles introduced.

1930 Truss rod underframing discontinued on 61 ft corridor stock.

1932 Cast steel open fronted axlebox adopted for freight stock.

December First all-welded wagon underframe introduced.
Wheelbase on open and mineral wagons increased from 9 ft to 10 ft.

1933 Tourist stock introduced.

1934 All-welded coach underframes introduced.
Fitted covered vans to be built on steel underframes.
Pressed steel ends introduced.

1935 Introduction of Class A4.
Introduction of 'Silver Jubilee' train.

1937 Revised layout of freight stock lettering.
Garter blue livery adopted for Class A4.
Stainless steel letters and numerals adopted for Class A4.
'Coronation' introduced.
'West Riding Limited' introduced.
'East Anglian' introduced.
Altered style of lettering introduced for freight stock.

1938 'Hook Continental' introduced.

1939 All-welded axlebox with pressed steel front adopted.
Revised numbering scheme for departmental stock introduced.

1940 Fitted freight stock livery changed to Bauxite.

1941 April   Death of Sir Nigel Gresley.
Edward Thompson appointed CME.
November Adoption of unlined black for locomotives.

1942 Part renumbering scheme carried out to clear way for Class B1.
July Lettering on locomotives reduced to 'N E'.

1943 Open and mineral wagons unpainted.
Renumbering scheme introduced but discontinued due to war.

1945 Thompson/Newton coach introduced.
All-steel open wagon introduced.

1946 Coaching stock renumbered.
Loco stock renumbered beginning 13/1/46.
Edward Thompson retired as CME, Arthur H. Peppercorn appointed.

1947 Loco renumbering scheme completed.
Formation of British Railways.

Appendix E — Running shed record

For those whose only contact with stream railways is through the many preserved lines it can be difficult to imagine what an everyday running shed contained. Of the many observations made by the late Mr J. G. Woodward, a random observation made on 5 March 1935 at King's Cross shed is reproduced here by kind permission of Mr Tony Sedgwick.

Class A1	2552	*Sansovino*
	2561	*Minoru*
	4472	*Flying Scotsman*
	4474	*Victor Wild*
	4475	*Flying Fox*
	4476	*Royal Lancer*
Class A3	2744	*Grand Parade*
	2750	*Papyrus*
Class A4	2510	*Quicksilver*

Class C1   3278, 3284, 3288, 4402, 4426, 4436, 4444, 4448, 4451 and 4458

Class D2   3049

Class J3   4039, 4060, 4099 and 4139

Class J6   3547, 3560, 3584, 3585, 3590, 3591, 3592

Class J52   3111, 3961, 3968, 3969, 3970, 3978, 4201, 4205, 4212, 4213, 4219, 4222, 4229, 4231, 4232, 4239, 4255, 4262, 4265, 4274, 4275, 4275, 4279, 4282, 4290

Class J57   3685

Class J69   7365

Class K2   4645, 4649, 4668 and 4679

Class K3   91, 112, 120, 143, 158, 163, 170, 204, 208, 229, 231, 2425, 2426, 2427, 2428, 2450, 2761 and 4009

Class N1   4554, 4575, 4579, 4581, 4583, 4596, 4599, 4600, 4601, 4602, 4604, 4605, 4606, 4607, 4609, 4610, 4611, 4612, 4613, 4614, 4615 and 4587

Class N2   4725, 4733, 4738, 4741, 4743, 4746, 4747, 4748, 4749, 4750, 4757, 4758, 4759, 4760, 4761, 4762, 4763, 4764, 4765, 4766, 4769 and 4770

Class N7   2650, 2662, 2663, 2665, 2667, 2669, 2670, 2671, 2672, 2673, 2675, 2678, 2679, 2681, 2682, 2683, 2686 and 2687

Class 02   3496 and 3498

TOTAL 143

It will be seen that the LNER was not all Pacifics, and the large number of tank locomotives should be noted.

Appendix F — The specialist groups

The LNER modeller and enthusiast is indeed fortunate in that a number of specialist groups exist, who between them represent all the constituent companies. These are:

The LNER Study Group

The GNR Society
The NER Association
The NBR Study Group
The GNoSR Association
The GCR Society
The GER Society
The M&GN Circle

Any of the above can be contacted through the editors of the model railway magazines, subject to the usual courtesies.

Appendix G — Bibliography

Historic Carriage Drawings in 4 mm Scale David Jenkinson & Nick Campling, Ian Allan,

Gresley's Coaches Michael Harris, David and Charles,

A Pictorial Record of LNER Wagons Peter Tatlow, Oxford Publishing Company,

A Pictorial Record of LNER Constituent Signalling A.A. Maclean, Oxford Publishing Company,

The London & North Eastern Railway Cecil J. Allen, Ian Allan,

A History of the LNER Michael R. Bonavia, George Allen & Unwin,
Part 1 The First Years, 1923–33
Part 2 The Age of the Streamliners, 1934–39
Part 3 The Last Years, 1939–48

Locomotives of the LNER Railway Correspondence & Travel Society,
Part 1   Preliminary Survey
Part 2A Tender Engines — Classes A1 to A10
Part 2B Tender Engines — Classes B1 to B19
Part 3A Tender Engines — Classes C1 to C11
Part 3B Tender Engines — Classes D1 to D12
Part 3C Tender Engines — Classes D13 to D24
Part 4   Tender Engines — Classes D25 to E7
Part 5   Tender Engines — Classes J1 to J37
Part 6A Tender Engines — Classes J38 to K5
Part 6B Tender Engines — Classes O1 to P2
Part 6C Tender Engines — Classes Q1 to Y10
Part 7   Tank Engines — Classes A5 to H2
Part 8A Tank Engines — Classes J50 to J70
Part 8B Tank Engines — Classes J71 to J94
Part 9A Tank Engines — Classes L1 to N19
Part 9B Tank Engines — Classes Q1 to Z5
Part 10 Miscellaneous Engines, Railcars and Statistics

Index